GOSPEL IN THE STADIUM

Taking the Gospel beyond the Church Wall

Samuel A. ALABI

GOSPEL IN THE STADIUM
Copyright © 2014 by Samuel A. Alabi

ISBN: 978-1-312-30816-9

Cover Design in Nigeria by **Moyosore Gbuyiro** +2348060084015

Published in the United States of America by

Lulu.

Lulu.com
3101 Hillsborough Street
Raleigh, NC 27607
United States

Contact the Author on
+234 803 049 7794 *and* +234 815 999 0308
E-mail: samalbs0881@gmail.com
Facebook: Samuel Ayantoye Alabi
Twitter: @SamuelAyantoyeA
"I am entrusted with the gospel to the uncircumcised" Galatians 2:7-8

First Edition, 2014

All Scripture quotations are from the New International Version of the Bible.

ALL RIGHTS RESERVED

No claims of absolute originality are made for this publication. As one man said, "I milk a lot of cows, I churn my own butter." Yet nothing in it may be reproduced for profit in any form or by any means —electronic, photocopying, recording, or otherwise- without the prior written permission from the copyright owner, except in the case of brief quotations in a review.

ENDORSEMENTS

The gospel could be made relevant on the football pitch and in the basketball hall. Olympic started in the city of Athens. Paul preached the gospel in this city and he made copious analogies in his letters to the church at Corinth using several sporting terms. We should not concede this land to the devil. We should teach sports men and women in our congregation how to make sports a platform through which people would encounter Jesus. I believe there should always be intersections of the Gospel with every other area of human existence . . . The author has expressed this passion in this book. I recommend this book for every sports-loving folk who desires the kingdom of this world to totally become the Kingdom of our God and of His Christ.
Rev. Gideon O. Akanbi, President, Godly Brains Ministries Intl., Ibadan, Oyo State, Nigeria

Many have lived with the misconception that sports had no place in Christianity. In this book, *Gospel in the Stadium,* Pastor Alabi strongly proves that sport is digging deep into the hearts of the people around us, changing church meeting settings, raising economies and gaining awesome grounds in the global world. He provides some fresh insights about an alternative mode to reach the hearts of people who are 'crazy' about sports (especially young people). That avenue is sport! Sports must no longer be regarded as a stool! As people called to make disciples of all nations, it will be unwise not to use sports as a tool! Every Pastor and Leader of young people must welcome this book not only unto their shelves but also into their core Ministry Practices. This is a-must-read book! Good work done Pastor Sam Alabi.
Rev. Clement K. Addo, National Coordinator, Youth & NUBS, Ghana Baptist Convention, Ghana

This is a wonderful and powerful book. It is full of fresh revelation of what God can do through Sport Evangelism. I hope this generation will take good advantage and explore this avenue to reach millions of souls for our Lord Jesus Christ! It is high time we all put down various strategies to depopulate the kingdom of Satan to populate the Kingdom of our Lord and of His Christ.
Rev. 'Banjo Ajao, Pastor, First Baptist Church, Kaduna, Kaduna State, Nigeria

No other single group seems better qualified than the youths to lead the crusade for spiritual renewal within the churches. The purpose of this book is therefore to challenge churches to take a new look at the ministry of the youths today... This book is designed to equip our Christian youths that will become the church's arms and legs doing everything necessary to help the church grow and develop links with its local community... This book is biblically based and I recommend it to every church, pastor, Christian youths and theological institutions for personal reading, for seminars and workshops organized for Christian youths in the Church, Associations and Conferences. I also recommend it as a reference material for every church Library.
Rev'd Prof. Joseph Abiodun Ilori, Former President, Nigerian Baptist Theological Seminary, Ogbomoso.

DEDICATION

To God Almighty for His anointing for exceptional pastoral ministry in the postmodern world

To my wife, Funmilayo, for her understanding of my unique pastoral ministry

To my children, Emmanuel and Israel, for believing in my unique pastoral ministry

ACKNOWLEDGEMENT

"My soul glorifies the Lord and my spirit rejoices in God my Saviour, for He has been mindful of the humble state of His servant. From now on all generations will call me blessed, for the Mighty One has done great things for me- holy is His name" (Luke 1: 46b - 49).

I thank God for everyone who has contributed to the success of this work in one way or the other, pages of this book cannot be sufficient to write your names in appreciation. May the Lord appreciate you all and bless the works of your hands in Jesus' name.

I am however going to single out my fathers in the Lord, the erstwhile General Secretary of the Nigerian Baptist Convention, Rev. S. Ademola Ishola (PhD) and the erstwhile President of the Nigerian Baptist Theological Seminary Ogbomoso, Rev. Prof. Joseph Abiodun Ilori, for appreciation. It has always been my dream to have them contribute to my book, and this has come true by their willingness to write the Foreword and Preface (respectively) to this book. Daddies, you are true models and I say thank you sirs. May you both remain relevant and ageless in God's agenda for this generation in Jesus' name.

My wife, Funmilayo, and my children, T'Oluwani and AyanfeOluwa have been my encouragers. May the Lord prosper His work in our hands together in Jesus' name.

Lastly, I acknowledge all authors whose materials I used in the course of this work, may you all not be empty of divine inspirations in Jesus' name. Thank you all and God bless.

Samuel A. ALABI
*Youth & Students' Ministries Department,
Baptist Building,
Ibadan, Nigeria.
9th June, 2014*

CONTENTS

Endorsements	3
Dedication	5
Acknowledgement	6
Contents	8
List of Figures	10
Foreword	11
Preface	16
Introduction	21

SECTION 1: SPORTS

1. Definition of Sports	27
2. Historical Background to Sports	30
3. Types of Sports	38

SECTION 2: SPORTS MINISTRY

4. Definition of Sports Ministry	51
5. Historical Background to Sports Ministry	61
6. Benefits of Sports Ministry	70
7. Challenges of Sports Ministry	75

SECTION 3: THE ROLE OF THE CHURCH

8. Theology of Sports	85
9. Starting Sports Ministry in the Local Church	90
10. Basic Needs for Sports Ministry	99
11. A Coded Gospel	105
12. Upholding Christian Virtues as an Athlete	113
13. Reaction to Sporting Activities on Sundays	123
Conclusion	140
Appendix: How to Start Sports Ministry in Schools	143
Index	149
Bibliography	156
Notes	160

LIST OF FIGURES

Figure 1: Philosophy of Sports Ministry — 54

Figure 2: Purpose of Sports Ministry — 58

Figure 3: Benefits of Sports Ministry — 74

Figure 4: Challenges of Sports Ministry — 78

Figure 5: Theology of Sports — 86

Figure 6: How to Start Sports Ministry in the Local Church — 91

Figure 7: Basic Needs for Sports Ministry — 100

Figure 8: Guide to Error-Free Sports Ministry — 103

Figure 9: Upholding Christian Virtues in Athletes — 120

Figure 10: The Right Way to Participate in Sports — 129

Figure 11: Result of Discipleship — 132

Figure 12: Christianity as a 3D-Relationship — 136

FOREWORD

I remember "shocking" some pastors at a retreat with a statement on whether it would not be necessary to ask all our Royal Ambassadors and the Lydia's (Auxiliary) in our churches to dress for football game on a Sunday and to ask them to go and play ball with some boys whose pastime is playing soccer on Sunday mornings. I also asked whether it would not be expedient for the girls, in the name of the Lord to serve the boys soft drinks after the games. The goal of the outing for the young people is to lead some of the boys to join the church of the young players and servers some of the Sundays! I realize that Sunday after Sunday, we, the *salt of the world* are packed inside the saltshaker—the church building when we ought to be sprinkled around the neighborhood where our church is planted or located. In other words, it should not be strange for any congregation to close our doors on some Sunday mornings and get out walking around our neighborhood and sharing the Word and any substance of worth with those who live in the community. One can imagine the impact of such practice on some people in the neighborhood. What is the relevance of a church in any neighborhood that the neighbors do not feel her presence? How can a church be surrounded by unbelievers and yet they do not even feel her presence?

The book, *Gospel in the Stadium,* may be a serious parable for many of our churches; yet, it is a clarion call for us to engage in paradigm shift from what has become a tradition that must not be broken. The strange words, "we have never done it that way before" may need to be changed around. We need to try some things that sound strange—engaging in soccer match with another church of different tradition for instance, and to ask all our neighbors to come and watch on one Sunday morning. Perhaps around 11 O'clock in the morning till noon, and then provide soft drinks and snacks for all the spectators who may be mostly our friends and relatives who live in the community where the churches are located. The goal is for a worship to be held in front of "strangers" who may not be familiar with church traditions, and to offer them opportunity to hear the Gospel preached thereafter.

Sports have become serious gods that some people worship on Sundays, and this may continue to be so given the forces of economics behind them. The media of all types are involved. Business men and women who make serious money from sports are behind it. Advertising companies, beverage and food vendors, hotels, transport companies, just to mention few businesses are making sporting activities one major economic force that provides several million-job opportunities. What then can the Church do to be in contact with the several millions of people waiting to hear the Gospel and not in our familiar places—church buildings? How can we package the Good News in such a way that will rival *Coca Cola* or similar soft drink companies? Sporting activities can grant us necessary audience to more people than we can imagine. The schools are one of the main targets—providing sporting items for some schools and providing them enabling environment for them to exercise their bodies.

We can beautify the neighborhood's playing ground and serve as church-patrons, and even sponsor some sporting activities with our money and material resources. Old people's homes, hospitals, orphanages, prisons, students' camps, including Youth Corps camping ground are some avenues or places where the churches can touch lives through sporting activities. It is high time churches started to extend calls to *Youth Pastors*—male and female who may be given sporting orientation as to provide sporting opportunities for all categories of our members and our neighbors in particular.

The author has provided ideas as to how we can make good use of sports to share the Good News of our Lord Jesus Christ. I fully recommend this book for all our pastors, youth leaders, men and women leaders who will find the contents helpful in organizing sporting activities in the local churches. It can even be used for small group Bible study for in-depth discussions. When sportsmanship is wrapped in *Christmanship*, that is, when we make good use of every opportunity sporting activities open up to us with the nature and character of the Lord, we can then share the Good News in the power of the Holy Spirit. We may be surprised as to how many the Lord will add to our numbers, even neighbors who would have considered the Church odd place to belong! May the Lord use the contents in this book to awaken the Church to vast opportunities sports can provide as avenues to preach the Gospel to all and sundry.

Rev. S. Ademola Ishola, PhD
Former General Secretary,
Nigerian Baptist Convention,
13th May, 2014.

PREFACE

No one person ever writes a book. One individual may write the manuscript, but the concepts are hammered out through years of reading and conversation. A chance remark by a total stranger or a sentence in the morning paper sometimes strikes home and stimulates an idea.

Most books evolve rather than burst forth, in full regalia. This Book, **GOSPEL IN THE STADIUM**, is through intense discussions with many pastors and church leaders across the nation. In recent years, many church leaders have sensed the need for a nucleus of committed persons to lead churches to become dynamic witnessing and ministering fellowships. No other single group seems better qualified than the youths to lead the crusade for spiritual renewal within the churches. The purpose of this book is therefore to challenge churches to take a new look at the ministry of the youths today. According to the author of this book, Sport Ministry takes its mission from the words of Jesus in **Luke 4: 18**. There in the synagogue in his hometown, Jesus quotes the words of Isaiah: "The spirit of the Lord is on me, because he has anointed me to preach good news to the poor. He has sent me to proclaim freedom for the prisoners and recovery of sight for the blind, to release the oppressed, to proclaim the year of the Lord's favour." Based on the quotation the author believes that the mission of the Youth/Sport Ministry is not just to talk about what to do but to demonstrate the Christian faith by actually doing it. The author clearly demonstrates how the youths through Sport Ministry can show faith at work. Many people see the Christian faith as merely a set of beliefs, a collection of ideas, which do not actually have to be turned into action. However, if Christian faith is to be more than an empty word, it must demonstrate a holistic gospel – a gospel that is for body, soul and spirit. This book is designed to equip our Christian youths that will become the church's arms and legs doing everything necessary to help the church grow and develop links with its local community. This book discusses clearly the basic tenets of sport ministry, which include communicating the gospel effectively not just about talking to people but through actions. Through Sports Ministry, youths have opportunity to spend time for training through a detailed and thorough lecture and seminar programmes. Through these programmes, they learn new skills and put them into practice. This book shows clearly that Christian youths have all kinds of backgrounds and have different levels of experience. Some are students; some are workers while many are degree holders. The one thing they have in common is a desire to get involved with the nitty-gritty of Church life. Sport ministry provides an opportunity for the youths to learn not only on how to give their time to God through the local church but also how God can speak to them about their future. Many youths through sport ministry have discovered gifts and skills, which they have on to develop in the future. This book emphasizes the belief that it is vital to give youths the opportunity to exercise gifts and take responsibilities. Only then do they really start to learn and grow. This is what the Sport Ministry does and stands for. The book is divided into three sections and has thirteen chapters including the following: Historical Background of Sports and Sports Ministry, Definition of key terms, Types of Sports, Benefits of Sport Ministry, Theology of Sports Ministry, How to start a Sport Ministry in the church, Expected Christian virtues from Christian youth Athletes. In this practical guide to the understanding and practicing of sport ministry, the author offers refreshing insights into the ways that Christian youths can and should be involved in spreading the good news of Jesus through sports and sport ministry. While not all Christians are called and gifted to become evangelists, we are all called to promote the gospel through a wide range of activities – prayer, financial partnership, good deeds, godly lives, daily conversation, sports and Sports Ministry – with and without our lips. This book is biblically based and I recommend it to every church, pastor, Christian youths and theological institutions for personal reading, for seminars and workshops organized for Christian youths in the Church, Associations and conferences. I also recommend it as a reference material for every church Library.

Finally, I commend the effort of Pastor Toye Alabi (author) for producing this quality material for our Christian youths.

Rev'd Prof. Joseph Abiodun Ilori,
Former President,
Nigerian Baptist Theological Seminary,
Ogbomoso.
9th June, 2014

INTRODUCTION

"I am not ashamed of the gospel, because it is the power of God for the salvation of everyone who believes: first for the Jew, then for the Gentile" (Romans 1:16).

Nigeria's largest unreached people group is the **youth**. Many youth are becoming more dissatisfied with the church and things of God by the day. A minimum of 50% of the congregation of any church in this contemporary time comprises of children and youth, which implies that the future of this nation and the church lies in the spiritual upbringing of these young ones. There are, at least, three things competing for the place of God in the life of the contemporary youth and they are **Music**, **Media** and **Sports** (MMS). The focus, however, in this piece is on Sports; how to help the contemporary Christian youth and pastors understand God's perspective to sport and how to use it to propagate the gospel of Jesus Christ.

On Sunday **February 10, 2013**, during the morning worship, the Pastor of a Nigerian Baptist Church said to his congregation,

> "As we all know, the Super Eagles of Nigeria will be playing with their counterparts from Burkina-Faso in the final of the Orange African Cup of Nations tonight at 7:30. Therefore, our evening worship today will start at 5pm as usual, but there will be no Discipleship lifestyle programme. We will begin the worship at 5pm and try to finish on or before 7pm so that we can all return to our various houses to watch the match."

After the pastor's announcement, many questions ran through my mind at the same time including the following:

- Should the church introduce physical activities into her spiritual activities?
- How can sports be relevant to the **gospel**?
- To what extent should the church be involved in sports?

- How could the church reach the young ones who are playing sports on Sunday morning in her community?

It was a privilege to teach a course on Sports Ministry during the January 2014 Minimester programme at the Nigerian Baptist Theological Seminary, Ogbomoso. In the course of the class, I gave out a questionnaire to the student pastors in the class I taught to administer. The questionnaire was adapted from the M.Th. thesis of Timothy Tucker submitted to the South African Theological Seminary on Practical Theology. The responses of these student pastors revealed to me that there are (still) many misconceptions about Sports Ministry in the (Baptist) church. The responses of the student pastors revealed that Nigerian Baptist Pastors (and perhaps Nigerian Pastors generally) do not really understand what sports ministry is all about or they are yet to device how to initiate or start Sports Ministry in their respective local churches, and with many believing that it could be a distraction from spiritual life.

One doctrine that seems to have done more harm than good to the church, in church history, is the **doctrine of dualism**. This doctrine teaches separation between spiritual/sacred and secular things. It has also affected Christians' participation in politics and other secular activities in the world at large. It is time the church balanced between spiritual/sacred and secular things rather than separate them.

How could Christians be the light of the world as Christ commanded if we remain separate from the world (Matthew 5:14-16)? How could the church positively affect the sports-minded people in her community for Christ if she remains separate from sporting activities? It is time we arose as a church to neutralize the bad effect of the doctrine of dualism on the mindset of average Christians in the contemporary time.

SECTION 1
SPORTS

"For by (Christ) all things were created: things in heaven and on earth, visible and invisible, whether thrones or powers or rulers or authorities; all things were created by Him and for Him" (Colossians 1:16).

Sport is one of the three foremost unifying languages presently in the world, which the church needs to learn how to use to communicate the gospel effectively to the contemporary generation. The other two are Music and Media (as mentioned earlier); however, the focus here is on Sport.

Interestingly, God did create sport (and these other two) as He gave the idea to the people who invented it. The fact that many people are abusing sport and some of these other secular activities in the world (like Music, Media, Internet and others) do not deny the truth that God through Christ created all things for His purpose and His glory.

CHAPTER ONE

DEFINITION OF SPORTS

Etymologically, sport means 'leisure', deriving its origin from an old French word *disport*.[1] In the beginning, the church had influence in developing sports. However, the church was not stable in her interplay with sport (relative details in section two), which had original credibility through the church.[2]

Sports exist in their hundreds, from those either requiring only two participants, up to those with hundreds of simultaneous participants, in teams or competing as individuals.[3] Wikipedia defines it as "all forms of competitive physical activity, through casual or organized participation, aim to use, maintain or improve physical abilities and provide entertainment to participants."[4] However, this definition may not be thorough because there are times when doing sports may not necessarily have anything to do with competition but exercise and/or recreation. In the same vein, sport does not only provide entertainment to participants but also to spectators of the game worldwide.

The National Sports Policy of Nigeria in 2009 defined sports as "physical and social activities done according to rules for exercise, competition or recreation."[5] I would have preferred the National Sports Policy of Nigeria's definition of sports but for some few things not added.

Therefore, considering the two definitions (above), I have defined sports as *all forms of physical and social activities done according to rules for exercise, competition or recreation purposely to build, maintain or improve physical, mental and/or social abilities and provide entertainment to both participants and spectators*. In other words, the essence of doing sports includes building, maintaining and/or improving good physique, psychology and relationship.

Baseball, rugby, football (known as soccer in the US), athletics and the likes are examples of sports that improve physical abilities of participants, while the likes of scrabble, chess, snooker, 'ludo' among others are examples of sports that primarily improve the mental abilities of participants. However, all sporting activities contribute to building and maintaining good relationship, depending on participants and spectators.

There are rules that govern different sports to ensure fair competition, and allow consistent adjudication of the winner. Wikipedia affirms that "winning (in sports) can be determined by physical events such as scoring goals or crossing line first, or by the determination of judges who are scoring elements of the sporting performance or artistic impression.[6]"

CHAPTER TWO
HISTORICAL BACKGROUND TO SPORTS

Ancient Greece with the first Olympic Games in 776BC introduced formal Sports to the entire world.[7] At that time, Olympic was "just a one-day athletic meeting with a single competitive event."[8] However, the history of sports probably extends as far back as the existence of man.[9] Other competitive events like discus and javelin throwing, long jump, boxing, wrestling, chariot and horse racing among others were added to the Olympic Games in the 7th century BC.[10] In the 6th century BC, Polo and Hockey emerged from Persia and Athens respectively and gained recognition as Olympic Games.[11]

Greek boxers, in the 4th century, became more hostile to their opponents when they replaced their soft leather fist-coverings with hard thongs. These hard thongs protected the fist but did "much greater damage to the opponent's face."[12] The ancient Olympic Games that began in 776BC lasted until AD393 when they were "abolished by a decree of the Christian emperor Theodosius."[13] By that time, the Olympic had been in uninterrupted existence for more than 1000 years.

Chess, "the greatest of all board games"[14] began to develop gradually in India by the 6th century AD. It was adopted in Persia, and "the Persian and Arabic term for the end of the game subsequently entered the languages of the world. *Shah Mat*, meaning 'the king is dead', becomes checkmate."[15]

During the Medieval period (1200-1485), people had little time or energy for sporting activities. Leisure time activities were confined to feast days. Games were local in nature such that each village had its own traditional activities. The government, from time to time, would ban these traditional activities in favour of archery training.[16] This implies that there were limitations to participation in sporting activities in different communities at this period with emphasis on professional training for people living at this time.

In the period of Tudor and Stuart (1485-1714), traditional folk games and activities flourished. Puritanism greatly reduced the opportunities to play and types of activity allowed. There was revival for traditional activities after the restoration in 1660, and sport moved away from its link with merrymaking.[17] In other words, sport at this period had no link with fun, as sporting activities were not synonymous to merrymaking.

The government in Hanoverian period (1714-1790) largely ignored play and sport. Individual people of all classes enjoyed their leisure to the full though. Increasing industrial and economic developments demanded regular working patterns and there was pressure for Sunday to be declared a Sabbath day. Large gatherings for sports often meant social malady, and regular, organized, rule-governed sport on a national scale emerged.[18]

The period known as "Changing times" (1790-1830) was not friendly with the world of sport at all. Traditional sport was under attack from all sides. Factory owners wanted a regular working week. Property owners feared the damage caused by large crowds. Churches criticized idleness, drunkenness and slack morality. Commercialization of sports developed, especially in horseracing, cricket and prize fighting.[19] This period made participation in sporting activities very difficult for people.

The history of organized sports in the United States of America began with the New York Knickerbockers in the 1840s.[20] Alexander Cartwright (1820-1892) who hailed from New York City was the leader of this New York Knickerbocker Base Ball Club whose members comprised professional men from all works of life –doctors, lawyers, engineers and well-to-do industrialists.[21] This man, Alexander Cartwright, invented the modern baseball field in 1845. He, together with the members of his Base Ball Club devised "the first rule and regulations that were accepted for the modern game of baseball."[22]

Scotland is a European country that has laid claim to the Invention of a number of popular international sports which include golf, rugby, tennis, curling, and of course football[23]. History has it that a Scotsman, William

McGregor, set up the first English football league, and "it was in Scotland in 1872 that the first international match was played in Patrick, Glasgow, where England and Scotland drew 0-0."[24]

In December of 1891, a trained 29years old pastor James Naismith, Scottish by origin but Canadian by birth, invented basketball. He had planned to become a minister and went ahead to study Theology at the Seminary. However, God did not direct him "to the pulpit but the basketball court."[25] Dr. James Naismith initially had nine people each side playing basketball until 1895 when basketball was regulated to five players aside. Basketball, an indoor game, came to being because of the challenge "of the brutal New England winters."[26] Naismith's interest was not necessarily in the game but in the Christian lives of the players of the game.[27]

SPORTS FROM 20TH CENTURY

Twentieth and twenty-first centuries wrote different stories in the history of sports in the whole world. Organized sporting involvement expanded rapidly across all classes between 1901 and 1918. The different classes played their sport separately. Public school athleticism dominated sport. Influence of male working class increased, notably in football in England and rugby in Wales. However, working class women were largely excused from sporting activities.[28]

May 21 1904 was an unforgettable date in the history of the Federation Internationale de Football Association (FIFA). Eight European nations –France, Belgium, Denmark, Netherlands, Spain, Sweden and Switzerland- came together in the rear of the headquarters of the Union Francaise de Sports Athletiques at the Rue Saint Honore 229 in Paris, France to start the body.[29]

Between the World Wars (1918-1940), there was steady growth in sports participation for all classes of society, although working class were least involved. Football continued to increase in popularity and by 1930s; it was the most popular sporting activity.[30] The FIFA World Cup was not that popular in its first (tentative) edition that started on July 18, 1930 in Uruguay.[31] However, since the competition began, it has constantly grown in popularity and prestige over the years.[32] Lack of facilities became an issue, particularly when national teams failed. There was little government involvement in sports, apart from physical education in schools. School physical education moved from therapeutic exercises to creative physical training. Commercialization of sport expanded rapidly, especially the provision for spectator sport.[33]

From 1940 until date, improved standard of living has enabled greater participation in sports for most social groups. Amateur administrators only reluctantly allowed commercial forces to enter the world of sports. Professional sports people had a long battle to be given fair rewards. Television attention increased in importance for sports and the sponsors. Physical education was established in the 1944 Act for its educational value. It moved away from educational value towards physical recreation and more recently towards health-related fitness. Various academic qualifications in physical education like B.Ed., GSE, GCSE, A-level and post-graduate studies stimulated scrutiny of the subject. Physical Education is now established in national curriculum as a foundation subject. There has been an increasing influence of market forces on schools, physical education, sporting facilities and sports.34

CHAPTER THREE
TYPES OF SPORTS

In all, the following are some of different kinds of sports (in alphabetical order) that we presently have around the world:

S/N	SPORTS
1	Aerobics
2	Aikido (Self-Defense)
3	Archery
4	Badminton
5	Ballet
6	Baseball
7	Basketball
8	Billiards
9	Boot Camp
10	Boot hockey
11	Bowling
12	Bridge
13	Broomball

14	Camping
15	Canoe Club
16	Cheerleading
17	Chess
18	Cricket
19	Curling
20	Cycling (road & mountain)
21	Disc Golf
22	Dog Racing
23	Drag Racing
24	Drill Team
25	Duathlon Training
26	Egg and Spoon Race
27	Elephant Polo
28	Equestrian
29	Exercise Class
30	Fishing
31	Fist ball
32	Fitness

33	Floor Hockey
34	Foosball
35	Free diving
36	Gate ball
37	Golf
38	Gymnastics
39	Handball
40	Hiking
41	Hockey
42	Hunting
43	Hurdles
44	Hurling
45	Ice Hockey
46	Ice Skating
47	Indoor Cricket
48	Indoor Soccer
49	In-line Skating
50	Javelin
51	Judo
52	Karate

53	Kickboxing
54	Kids game
55	Kung Fu San Soo
56	Lawn Bowls
57	Long Jump
58	Marathon
59	Mat Ball
60	Motorcycling
61	Motorsports
62	Netball
63	Nordic skiing
63	Paintball
64	Paralympics football
65	Pilates
66	Ping Pong (Table Tennis)
67	Polo
68	Power legs
69	Pro Wrestling
70	Racquetball
71	Referee Class

72	Rock Climbing
73	Roller Blading
74	Roller Hockey
75	Roller Skating
76	Rugby Football
77	Running
78	Sailing
79	Scrabble
80	Scuba Diving
81	Skateboarding
82	Snow Skiing
83	Snooker
84	Soccer (Football)
85	Softball
86	Stretching
87	Surfing
88	Swimming
89	T-Ball
90	Taekwondo
91	Tennis

92	Track and Field
93	Triathlon Training
94	Ultimate Frisbee
95	Underwater Football
96	Video Games
97	Volleyball
98	Walking
99	Wallyball
100	Water-skiing
101	Weight Lifting
102	Wheelchair racing
103	White-water river rafting
104	Winter Sports
105	Wrestling
106	Yoga
107	Youth Olympics[35]

However, because some of these sporting events are not common in Nigeria, the following fifteen are the ones popular in Nigerian Universities as recognized by the Nigerian Universities Games Association (NUGA)[36]

1. **Athletics**: This is the sport of competing in track and field events, including running races and various competitions in jumping and throwing.

2. **Badminton**: It is a game with rackets in which shuttlecock is hit back and forth across a net.

3. **Basketball**: This is a game played between two teams of five players in which goals are scored by throwing a ball through a netted hoop fixed at each end of the court.

4. **Chess**: It is a board game of strategic skill for two players, played on a chequered board on which each playing piece is moved according to precise rules. The object is to put the opponent's king under a direct attack from which escape is impossible (checkmate).

5. **Cricket**: This is a bat-and-ball game played between two teams of eleven players each on a field at the center of which is a rectangular 22-yard long pitch.

6. **Football**: It is any of various forms of team game of eleven players each, involving kicking (and in some cases also handling) a ball, in particular soccer or American football.

7. **Handball**: This is a game similar to fives, in which the ball is hit with the hand in a walled court.

8. **Hockey**: It is a team game played between two teams of eleven players each, using hooked sticks with which the players try to drive a small hard ball towards goals at opposite ends of a field. In North America, it is called *field hockey* to distinguish from *ice hockey*.

9. **Judo**: This is a sport of unharmed combat derived from *ju-jitsu* and intended to train the body and

mind. It involves using holds and leverage to unbalance the opponent.

10. **Squash**: It is a racquet sport played by two (singles) or four players (doubles) in a four-walled court with a small, hollow rubber ball.

11. **Swimming**: This is the sport or activity of propelling oneself through water using the limbs.

12. **Table Tennis**: It is an indoor game based on tennis, played with small bats and a ball bounced on a table divided by a net. It is otherwise known as Ping Pong.

13. **Taekwondo**: This is an art of self-defense that originated in Korea. It is the art of foot and hand striking.

14. **Tennis**: It is originally called *Lawn Tennis*. It is a game in which two or four players strike a ball with rackets over a net stretched across a court.

15. **Volleyball**: This is a game of two teams, usually of six players, in which a large ball is hit by hand over a high net, the aim being to score points by making the ball reach the ground on the opponent's side of the court.

SECTION 2
SPORTS MINISTRY

"... We are ... rebuilding the temple that was built many years ago, which a great king of Israel built and finished. But because our fathers had provoked the God of heaven to wrath, He gave them into the hand of Nebuchadnezzar king of Babylon, Chaldean, who destroyed this temple and deported the people to Babylon." Ezra 5:11-12

"I have other sheep, which are not of this fold; I must bring them also, and they will hear My voice; and they will become one flock with one shepherd" (John 10:16).

Sports Ministry is not sport per se, but God's perspective to sport. However, before we explore God's perspective to sport, it is needful to examine the history behind Sports Ministry in the life of the church (as I attempted for sports in the previous section).

Just like the biblical Jerusalem Temple that was destroyed by the Babylonian kingdom under Nebuchadnezzar, and was later rebuilt in the time of Ezra, so is the case with Sports Ministry. The ministry is not entirely a new idea to the church; it is only going through a rebuilding process in recent time, Ezra 5:11-12.

CHAPTER FOUR
DEFINITION OF SPORTS MINISTRY

WRONG PERCEPTIONS OF SPORTS MINISTRY

Many churches and/or Christians seem to be involved in Sports Ministry, but in the real sense of the word, they are far from doing ministry. Rather, they are participating in sports just as anybody or everybody who does not know Jesus Christ would participate in it. Many are just participating in sports for the FUN of it.

Sports Ministry is not just association between the Christian faith and sports. In other words, it is not bringing Christian rites and rituals to the playground like pre-game prayer rituals, providing alternative sporting activities within a Christian environment as a form of leisure, like a church family sports day, and theological schools separating a particular day of the week for sporting activities among others.

RIGHT PERCEPTIONS OF SPORTS MINISTRY

Sports Ministry (also referred to as Recreation Ministry or Activities Ministry[37]) is a ministry of Reconciliation in that

"God reconciled us to Himself through Christ and gave us the ministry of reconciliation" (2 Corinthians 5: 18 Paraphrased). It is supposed to bridge the gulf between the world of sports and the church of God. *Sports Ministry is to intentionally use one's sporting gift to glorify God and to extend His Kingdom on earth such that non-Christians would come to the saving knowledge of Jesus Christ through sport.* It seeks to glorify God in sport, thereby extending God's Kingdom on earth through sports (Colossians 3:17; 2 Peter 3:15).[38] Doing ministry through sports implies devoting oneself to God through Christ and people as much as devoting oneself to sporting activities.

It is important to note that the difference between the right and wrong perceptions of Sports Ministry is the **intention** for which one participates in sports. If the intention is other than soul winning and discipleship, then it is not ministry. In other words, before we can refer to our participation is sports as Ministry and not mere fun; it must include the following simultaneously according to Timothy Tucker:

a. **<u>Intentionally</u> Glorifying God in sport**: the reason and intention for participating in sports must always be for the glory to God.

b. **<u>Intentionally</u> Extending God's Kingdom through sport**: the reason and intention for participating in sports must be to proclaim the gospel of the Lord Jesus Christ.

c. **Sports Ministry <u>through the Church</u>**: Tucker's argument is that Sports Ministry is not a-one man business but what the entire church should do in agreement and unity, whereby every member of the church would know the vision and run with it.

d. **Sports Ministry as <u>a prophetic voice</u>**[39]: this actually implies that every member of the sport team, from the coach to all the players, would be the mouthpiece of God. In other words, as the Old Testament prophets spoke forth God's word and spoke for the Lord, every Christian athlete and coach should speak forth God's word and live for Him in their participation in sport.

PHILOSOPHY

Figure 1: Philosophy of Sports Ministry

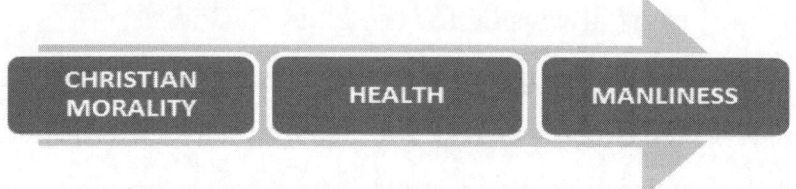

The philosophy of Sports Ministry is to encourage Christian morality, health and manliness while participating in sports. Christian morality in that Christians should not allow flesh and/or bad peer influence to dictate their behaviors while participating in sports on and off the pitch or playground. Health in that participating in sports reduces the risk of having certain health challenges such as Heart disease, Stroke, High Blood Pressure, Noninsulin-Dependent Diabetes, Obesity, Back Pain, Osteoporosis, and Old-Age Disability.[40] Manliness in that Christians should possess certain virtues for living such as Prudence, Temperance, Justice, Fortitude, Faith, Hope and Love in their participation in sports.[41] Therefore, one could refer to these virtues as

Christmanship; infecting the world of sports with the life of Christ.⁴²

VISION

The vision of sports ministry is to see a national or international movement of local churches participate in and/or support sporting and recreational activities to transform lives and reform societies for the Lord Jesus Christ. Churches, through pastors, should lead their sporting members to represent the interest of Christ in the corrupt world of sports.

MISSION

> *"When (Jesus) saw the crowds, He had compassion on them, because they were harassed and helpless, like sheep without a shepherd. Then He said to His disciples, 'The harvest is plentiful but the workers are few. Ask the Lord of the harvest, therefore, to send out workers into His harvest field'"* Matthew 9:36-38.

With respect to the passage in the gospel according to Matthew, churches that would make use of Sports Ministry must not only love God, but also love sports-minded people and the sports they play. This is what

Rodger Oswald referred to as serving God, serving the Church and serving the lost through sports.[43] Hence, the mission of sports ministry includes

- **Prayer**: this implies that the church should pray for the salvation of the erring ones in the world of sports. The church should also pray for the spiritual growth of the Christians amidst them. This kind of prayer is all encompassing.
- **Equip**: churches should be equipped with necessary trainings for teams leaders and teams members to accomplish the vision of Sports Ministry.
- **Empower**: local church Sports Ministry should be empowered with necessary sporting equipment and resource materials to accomplish the vision of the ministry.
- **Collaborate**: churches could collaborate with one another to embark on local and international mission trips, as sport is a good vehicle for mission action.

- **Play**: local churches should device means to play sports together with both Christians and non-Christians as a way of reaching out to them with the Gospel. This results to incarnation, relational or life-style evangelism.
- **Proclaim the Gospel**: in the course of playing with these non-Christians, Christians should device every means possible to share the gospel of the love of God to humanity such that those who have not accepted Him as Saviour and Lord might do so. Even though the emphasis in this book is on 'Demonstration of the gospel', we need not overlook the place and importance of proclaiming the gospel.
- **Disciple**: the church should device means to follow-up new converts on the playground such that they could become maturing Christians and thereby lighten the darkness in the world of sports.

PURPOSE

"Watch your life and doctrine closely. Persevere in them, because if you do, you will save both yourself and your hearers" (1 Timothy 4:16).

The purpose of sports ministry is to identify with the world of sports in relational and life-style evangelism with the intention of bringing non-Christians to the saving knowledge of Jesus Christ and a deeper relationship with the Lord that they might reform the society. In other words, the purpose of Sports Ministry is to

Figure 2: Purpose of Sports Ministry

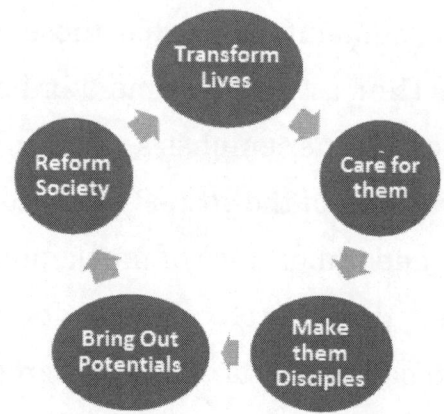

- **Transform Lives**: one can also refer to this as to win the lost for Christ by accommodating non-Christians (into our teams) and necessarily demonstrating Christ-likeness on regular basis as

we come together to exercise our bodies. This is known as relational evangelism.

- **Care for People**: this is the continuation of our evangelistic work. We would make it a habit to visit them in their homes at a regular interval and care for their wellbeing as well. This is especially the responsibility of the coach of the team.

- **Make Disciples**: this actually refers to relational discipleship. We would be consciously committed to making our team members grow spiritually by modeling the life of Christ to them.

- **Encourage Excellency**[44]: this refers to bringing out the best in the athletes. Everybody has potentials deposited in him/her; therefore, the church-based sports teams, through leaders or shepherd-coaches, should provoke the best out of the Christian athletes. Excellency should be a hallmark for every Christian athlete in his/her participation in world sports.

- **Reform Society**[45]: this would be possible by sending 'disciples' back into the 'harvest field' for fruitfulness. This does not mean that we would dispatch them from being in our team; it rather means that we would encourage them to demonstrate the life of Christ wherever they find themselves in their day-to-day activities and participation in sports in the society. However, it does not limit their fruitfulness to the field of play but to everyday works of life.

Interestingly, Sports Ministry does not achieve these five through the conventional evangelism and discipleship style, but through relationship, which is referred to as relational evangelism/discipleship.

CHAPTER FIVE
HISTORICAL BACKGROUND TO SPORTS MINISTRY

IN THE OLD TESTAMENT

The Old Testament period does not seem to have any connection with the history behind Sports Ministry. However, there are few biblical antecedents to sport in the Old Testament such as:

1Kings 18:16ff –talking about **contest** between Elijah and Prophets of Baal on Mount Carmel.

Psalm 78:72 –has traces of hand sports like tennis, handball, and volleyball among others.

Proverb 21:31 –could be linked with polo and order sports involving horse.

Ecclesiastes 9:11 –has traces of athletics, boxing, wrestling and the likes.

Isaiah 40:31b –has traces of athletics.

Jeremiah 12:5 –has traces of athletics, polo and other sports involving horses.

All these Bible passages (and few others not mentioned) are indications that 'sport' as a concept is not necessarily strange to the people who lived in the Old Testament era.

IN THE EARLY CHURCH

Sports Ministry generally can trace its roots to the early church, considering many analogies drawn from the world of sports by the Apostle Paul and a few other New Testament authors to illustrate Christian principles (Acts 20:24; 1 Corinthians 9:24-27; Galatians 2:2; Philippians 2:16; 3:14; 1 Timothy 1:18; 4:8; 6:12; 2 Timothy 4:7; Hebrews 12:1).[46] However, the church later, understandably and gradually, disengaged herself from sporting activities when "sport began to become more gruesome, and the Coliseum became a venue for sporting atrocities."[47] This implies that the early church later disengaged from participating in sports when sporting activities were no longer pleasant for church life.

IN THE MIDDLE AGES

Sports remained detached from the church from the early church era into the Middle Ages. In fact, the majority of church Fathers considered sport a distraction and hindrance to the move of God in the church.⁴⁸ Perhaps, that was the reason why the Christian emperor Theodosius in AD393 pronounced a decree to abolish the ancient Olympic Games.⁴⁹ In other words, the church in the Middle Ages perceived sport as sinful and preached separation between the church and the world –between spiritual/sacred and secular things, including sports. After all, *"What agreement is there between the temple of God and idols?"* 2 Corinthians 6:16a. This is the basis of the doctrine of dualism in the history of the church.

AT THE REFORMATION PERIOD

At the period of Reformation, the church was changing her attitudes towards sport, though she was still disengaged from sporting activities. Martin Luther (1484 - 1546), the brain behind Reformation, led the church back to Biblical teachings on matters such as justification by faith among others. John Garner in *Recreation and Sports Ministry* recorded that

> *"Luther . . . challenged the idea of pleasure being sinful. Prior to the Reformation, monks degraded their bodies in an attempt to glorify their soul . . . Luther argued*

> *against degrading the body: "God has indeed created body and soul and desires both to be allowed and give recreation, but with proper measure and purpose." Luther also spoke out for the participation in recreation. In a 1534 letter, he wrote, "To have pleasure in sins is of the devil, but participation in proper honourable pleasures with good and God-fearing people (are) pleasing to God"".*[50]

Luther categorically stated that pleasure is not necessarily sinful when we do it with the consciousness of and the fear of God. He, however, did not deny the possibility of pleasure being of the devil if tailored towards sin. Invariably, participating in sport, which is a form of pleasurable activity, may not necessarily be sinful if one does not allow the evil and atrocities attached to sport to overcome the fear and consciousness of God in one's life.

IN THE 19TH CENTURY

In the 19th century, there was a movement in the Great Britain known as *Muscular Christianity,* who brought a new dimension to Christians' perspective to sport. The movement has been traced to the efforts of Charles

Kingsley (clergyman, academic, novelist and poet) and his associate, Thomas Hughes (lawyer, politician and novelist) in the 1850s.[51] Clifford Putney defined Muscular Christianity as "a Christian commitment to health and manliness."[52] However, because the basic premise of this movement "was that participation in sport could contribute to the development of Christian morality, physical fitness, and 'manly' character,"[53] Muscular Christianity is better defined as *a Christian commitment to **morality**, health and manliness* (Emphasis added).

Social concerns of Muscular Christianity at that time included the protection of the weak, the plight of the poor, and the promotion of moral virtue.[54] This movement led to what the church now has as the contemporary Sports Ministry.

In the 1870s, churches sponsored majority of football clubs in England, like Southampton Football Club, Fulham Football Club and Queens Park Rangers Football Club.[55] The teachings of Muscular Christianity, once more, encouraged the church to identify with sport.[56] Consequently, "the Muscular Christianity movement . . .

greatly influenced world mission, and Muscular Missionaries travelled to Africa and beyond with a Bible in one hand, and a ball in the other."[57]

IN THE 20TH CENTURY

Early in the 20th century, the church, once again, began to disengage from sporting activities because sport was becoming more popular than the church and the things of God. It was as if the church's participation in sport had backfired. Timothy Tucker has this to say,

> *"The church embraced sport and saw it as a useful agent of change and as an opportunity to bring glory to God. Christians had even been used by God to increase the profile of sport and to promote its benefits for the common man. However, as the 19th Century closed and the new century began, sport became even more popular and powerful (than the church). As sports stars gained fame and fortune, the church began to turn its back on what it had previously embraced. The church viewed its embracing of sport as having been counter-productive. Sport was becoming popular at the expense of religion, with sport itself almost becoming a religion."*[58]

Unfortunately, what the 20th century church feared eventually caught up with her. Sport, in the contemporary world with effect from the 20th century, seems to be much stronger than faith and religion because no religion brings people of all ages, tribes, and sects together in a single moment as sport does. Indeed, sport is very powerful!

POST-WORLD WAR II EXPERIENCE

As the 20th century continued to disengage from sporting activities, it will be of interest to know that it was the aftermath of the Second World War, around the middle of the 20th century, which revealed the hidden power of sports to proclaim the Gospel of the redeeming grace of Jesus Christ. From the 1940s, the church in the United States of America led this movement as they

> *"started to re-engage with the world of sport, recognizing the potential of impacting the world for Christ through sports outreach . . . In Africa, the re-engagement process is presently underway, as full-time sports ministries view the sports field as an opportunity to reap a harvest of souls."*[59]

LISTS OF SOME INTERNATIONAL SPORTS MINISTRIES

The following International Sports Ministries are some of the ones established after the experience of the Second World War in the 1940s, and they have been raising many disciples in this respect around the world. There are well over 100 of them presently all over the world and they include[60]:

1. Sports Friends International (SFI)
2. Sports Outreach International (SOI)
3. Fellowship of Christian Athletes (FCA)
4. Athletes in Action (AIA)
5. Church Sports International (CSI)
6. Athletes in Christ (AIC)
7. Christians in Sports (CIS)
8. Association of Church Sports and Recreational Ministry (CSRM), and

9. Scripture Union Australia[61]

It is worthy of note on this point that these ministries (listed above) are not local churches or Christian denominations, they operate like Missionary Agencies with the willingness to partner with local churches or Christian denominations around the globe with the intention of diversifying and/or being creative with Christian ministries. Therefore, local churches or Christian denominations should not feel insecure or suspicious of collaborating with any of them for the furtherance of the Gospel of Jesus Christ.

Finally, we can conclude that Sports Ministry in the Church has not been consistent over the years. However, we can trace the origin of this ministry to the early church from the analogies of the Apostle Paul and a few other New Testament authors in their epistles to the church. Records from historical antecedents have also revealed that Sports Ministry had faced several challenges from both the church and the world, out of which the doctrine of dualism stands out.

CHAPTER SIX

BENEFITS OF SPORTS MINISTRY

The Royal Ambassador of Nigeria in a Nigerian Baptist Association started a football competition in December 2013 with the intention of making it an annual competition. The final of the maiden competition was played between the RA of First Baptist Church and the RA of Good News Baptist Church of the Association on 24 December at the Christ Apostolic Church Grammar School in a town in Osun State. Incidentally, my family was in the town to celebrate Christmas with my parents who are the under-Shepherd of the First Baptist Church. Therefore, I chose to watch the final match to encourage these young ones and (probably and formerly) introduce them to Sports Ministry, even as some leaders of Baptist churches in the Association would be present at the final match.

The match ended in a goalless draw after extra time, and on a lighter mood, the better side lost after a penalty shoot-out. The RA of the First Baptist Church won the final match by four goals to three (if I am not mistaken).

This is my point. In the course of the match, I noticed that faces of about three boys from the First Baptist Church RA team (which I am familiar with) were not familiar to me. I suspected they were not members of my father's church; they were what some people would refer to as 'mercenaries'. Alas! My guess what right. Some of the members of the other team wanted to protest after the match, claiming that the winner used mercenaries to play the match for victory. We later prevailed on the protest and we encouraged the players to learn how to accommodate one another.

When we got to church later that evening, I addressed the team and inquired if there were any of them who were not members of the church. These three boys indicated that they were not members of the church. Interestingly, they were Muslims! "Muslims inside the church? Playing football with the church RA team? This is unimaginable! It is simply incredible!" I reasoned to myself.

Anyone who is familiar with this town in Osun State would understand my personal rational argument. Muslims in the town roughly takes 70% of the entire population and they are repulsive and hostile to the Gospel. Hence, I was happy that three of them were willing to identify with their Christian friends on the field of play. I spoke with these guys, introduced Jesus Christ to them and I prayed with them. I also spoke with one of the RA boys whose Christian stand I could vouch for, to follow these boys up, invite them to play football more regularly and exemplify Christ to them and others on the field of play that more of them could accept Jesus as the Lord and Saviour.

There are a number of benefits, which the local church could derive from Sports Ministry, and they include but not limited to the following:

1. Sports Ministry can keep the church in touch with the society and make her culturally relevant.
2. It can contribute to 'body-life' and the fellowship aspect of the church.

3. It can keep young people from drifting from the church
4. It can help channel the energy of the young people into a useful venture, thereby keeping them out of trouble
5. It can provide an "entry-level" of service for new believers.
6. It can provide a place for teaching life skills and developing leaders.
7. It can give people a vision and heart for reaching the lost.
8. It can provide opportunities to plant cell groups, and ultimately plant churches.
9. Sports Ministry can help the church to cross or overcome cultural barriers and other barriers (religion, tribal) thereby extending greater influence in their community and engaging in mission.
10. It can assist the church in evangelism and fulfilling the Great Commission.

11. It can bring transformation and Kingdom values to the world of sports, thus redeeming what has become the "devil's domain".
12. It can help to reduce the risk of having certain health challenges in the body such as Heart disease, Stroke, High Blood Pressure, Noninsulin-Dependent Diabetes, Obesity, Back Pain, Osteoporosis, and Old-Age Disability.

Figure 3: Benefits of Sports Ministry

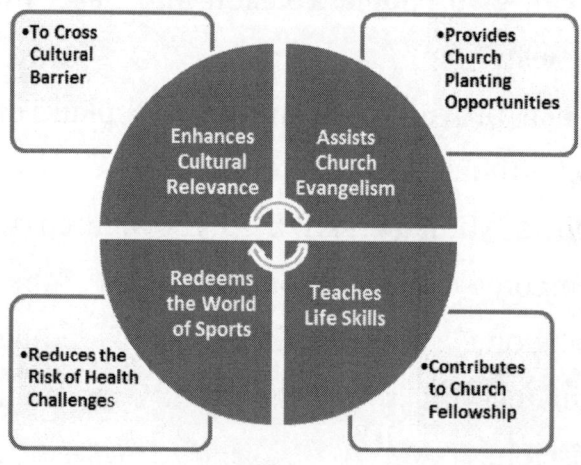

CHAPTER SEVEN
CHALLENGES OF SPORTS MINISTRY

I have interacted with a number of people, including pastors and nonprofessionals, on the subject of Sports Ministry in the Nigerian Baptist Convention. Unfortunately, local churches do not know that much is expected from them for Sports Ministry to really be what it is supposed to be. My heart bleeds whenever people enquire with expectation that the Sports Ministry Unit of the Nigerian Baptist Convention would start and be responsible to cater for Sports Ministry in local churches. Sports Ministry Unit cannot start Sports Ministry for any local church, it exists to collaborate with and put local churches through on how to go about the operation of the ministry.

In fact, in one of the several vision castings I went to do on Sports Ministry, two different categories of people approached me with different suggestions to move the ministry forward. One category said we should ensure that pastors subscribe into this vision for the ministry to have a breakthrough in various local churches, while the other category said it depends on how far we could carry the youth fellowship of the local church along that would determine its acceptability and breakthrough in the church and Convention at large. Many of these people came up with different ideas on how to come about the ministry in Nigeria, especially since the idea is strange and new to our Christian culture. Some even counseled that we should organize football competitions among conferences of the Nigerian Baptist Family and among churches of different denominations. Some said we could start with a number of churches in Ibadan Baptist Conference, while some out rightly opposed the idea of Sports Ministry, claiming that it is a distraction from spiritual life of the young ones in the church and society.

In short, the Sports Ministry is not without its various challenges in the church and in the society. Steve Connor referred to some of these challenges as the 'Past mistakes'[62] that made Sports Ministry lost its ground in God's agenda for it in the life of the church. The challenges include

- No cohesive, long-term plans for assimilating sports people into the church's fellowship.
- Not considering the long-term investment it would take to sustain a strategic ministry.
- No attainable goal setting to help Sports Ministry stays on course.
- The ministry's emphasis eroded from helping people grow in Christ to merely winning competitions.
- The church was not developing a proper infrastructure for sustainable ministry.
- The church was not adequately training Sports Ministry leaders or cultivating new leadership.
- The ministry was not casting a strategic vision for the church as a corporate Body.
- The church was getting involved in Sports Ministry for the wrong reasons.[63]

All these challenges given by Steve Connor are just four, according to Rodger Oswald, in that Sports Ministry is usually

i. Misunderstood,
ii. Unappreciated,
iii. Under-staffed, and
iv. Under-funded[64]

Figure 4: Challenges of Sports Ministry

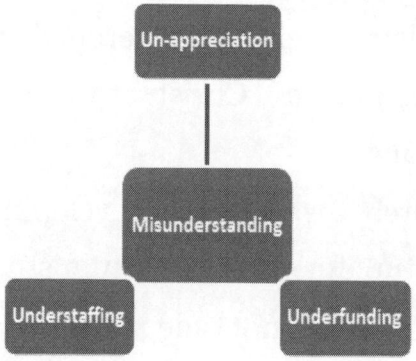

1. MISUNDERSTANDING

A pastor confessed that the very first time she saw me casting vision on Sports Ministry; she felt "what has sports got to do in the church when there are other salient and better things to discuss?" Christians often think of Sports Ministry as merely a game or an activity such that all through the year they are engaged by organizing one competition or the other. As much as organizing competitions are not bad on their own, the motive behind the organization of these competitions is what actually matters and which would determine the success of the ministry. As long as the motive for organizing any sporting competition is not on mission and evangelism, then Sports Ministry is misunderstood.

A young man also confessed that when he had about the first training the Sports Ministry Unit of the Nigerian Baptist Convention organized in collaboration with Sports Friends Nigeria, he thought it was a screening exercise to recruit professional footballers by foreign (European) club side. Hence, he went to borrow money to buy a pair of soccer boot to attend the 'screening exercise'. However, he was disappointed when he got to the venue and discovered we were doing something different entirely from what he expected. No wonder he did not practice what he learnt in the training; he actually misunderstood the concept of Sports Ministry, he wanted to travel abroad to pursue his professional football career. Mind you, Sports Ministry is by no means against pursuing professional football career abroad; however, the focus is to transform the lives of young athletes in the society through the local church for them to reform the society. It is a ministry for the grassroots.

2. UN-APPRECIATION

Sports Ministry is not appreciated among some quarters in the church majorly because of the havoc of the doctrine of dualism on the church. Christians often classify sporting activities as secular and not sacred hence claiming it could be a distraction from spiritual life, especially for the youth. Unfortunately, this is common with pastors and church leaders who accuse their youth of being worldly and/or carnal for participating in sporting activity. Therefore, they devalue, discourage or run down Sports Ministry in their churches.

As an undergraduate, I used to have a music pastor who would (unnecessarily) extend choir rehearsals because he did not want us to go and watch the Barclays Premier League matches, claiming that we would be carried away by the frivolities of the matches, though many of us (including me) would sneak out of the rehearsal to watch 'star' matches. I am afraid if 'my music pastor' would appreciate or even encourage Sports Ministry in his church.

3. UNDER-STAFFING

In our context in Nigeria, under-staffing Sports Ministry is an understatement. We do not even have any place for Sports Ministry in our local churches. It is time for churches in Nigeria to see ministry beyond the four walls of the local church for us to be relevant to the challenges of this generation. Churches who could not manage a full-fledge Sports Ministry could merge the emerging Sports Ministry of the church to the established Mission and Evangelism team of the church such that they could work in collaboration for the propagation of the Kingdom of God. However, ministers (not necessarily pastors) in the Mission and Evangelism team must have or agree with the vision and be given proper orientation on how to make use of sport as a tool for ministry.

4. UNDER-FUNDING

Once a ministry is misunderstood, unappreciated and understaffed, it would naturally be underfunded because it would make no sense to the church leadership. The aforementioned three challenges have contributed to the slow pace at which churches are embracing and investing in Sports Ministry. Many believe that sustaining a Sports Ministry would require a lot of money. It is worthy of note at this junction that funding a Sports Ministry does not necessarily need to cost much. I have addressed this in details in the next section of this book.

SECTION 3

THE ROLE OF THE CHURCH

"How deserted lies the city, once so full of people! How like a widow is she, who once was great among the nations! She who was queen among the provinces has now become a slave. Bitterly she weeps at night, tears are upon her cheeks. Among all her lovers there is none to comfort her; they have become her enemies. After affliction and harsh labour, Judah has gone into exile. She dwells among the nations; she finds no resting place. All who pursue her have overtaken her in the midst of her distress" (Lamentations 1:1-3).

"You are the light of the world. A town built on a hill cannot be hidden. Neither do people light a lamp and put it under a bowl. Instead, they put it on its stand, and it gives light to everyone in the house. In the same way, let your light shine before others, that they may see your good deeds and glorify your Father in heaven" (Matthew 5:14-16).

"Going on from that place, (Jesus) went into their synagogue, and a man with a shriveled hand was there. Looking for a reason to accuse Jesus, they asked Him, 'Is it lawful to heal on the Sabbath?' He said to them, 'if any of you has a sheep and falls into a pit on the sabbath, will you not take hold of it and lift it out? How much valuable is a man than a sheep! Therefore, it is lawful to do good on the sabbath'" (Matthew 12: 9-12).

CHAPTER EIGHT

THEOLOGY OF SPORTS

David W. Cunningham coined the word *"sportsology"* as a terminology and only described it as 'A Theology of Sports' in one of his articles titled *Sports and the Christian*.[65] He argued that sport is not necessarily sinful. This he said to agree with different analogies in the Scriptures comparing the Christian journey with sporting activities. Cunningham said, ". . . If Paul in anyway deemed athletics to be sinful he surely would not have used them to illustrate the Christian life."[66] He however, noted that the attitude of Christian athletes or spectators of sports would determine whether it would be an offense to God. In other words, sport is neutral; it is in the same category with the likes of hotel, television, internet, money, computer and other products of civilization. It is neither good nor bad, depending on the condition of the heart of the athlete, the coach or the supporter.

Therefore, sportsology could be defined as *participating in or supporting sports not at the expense of worship to God but in reverence and acknowledgement of God whether one (or one's team) wins or not.* This definition implies the following two things:

❖ Whether one is an athlete, a coach or a spectator, one must not do it at the expense of one's worship to God. One's priorities as a Christian in the world of sports should, as a matter of fact, be underlined and informed by:

Figure 5: Theology of Sports

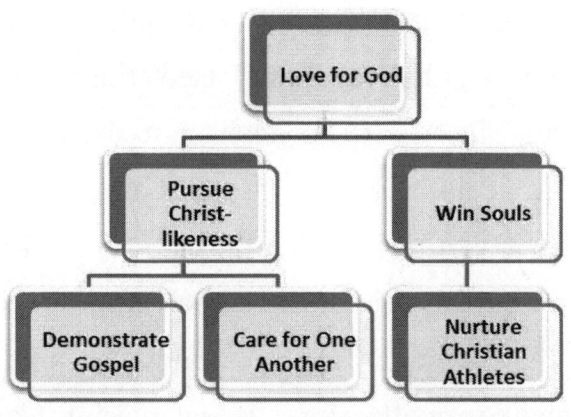

i. **Love for God**: Loving the Lord God with all the heart, soul, mind, and strength is not negotiable (Mark 12:30).

ii. **Pursuance of Christ-likeness**: Pursuing and practicing Christ-likeness while playing, coaching and/or supporting sporting activities (Philippians 1:21; 1 John 2: 28-29).

iii. **Soul Winning**: Evangelizing the lost souls in the world of sports should be the intention for which one participates in sports in any capacity (Acts 1:8; Matthew 28:19-20; Luke 24: 46-48).

iv. **Nurturing Christian Athletes**: Building up and discipling other believers in the world of sports should be our commitment (1 John 1:7; 1 Thessalonians 5:11; Matthew 28:19-20).

v. **Caring for One Another**: we build and keep earthly relationships that glorify God and manifest that we are children of God (1 John 2:9-11; Luke 15: 4-10).

vi. **Demonstrating the Gospel**: we must indicate our knowledge and understanding of God's Word by applying it to our day-to-day living, even on the playground (Psalm 119:11; 2 Timothy 2:15; 3:16-17).

❖ As one plays, coaches and/or supports sports, one must glorify God whether one wins or one loses. Many people in sports (Christians inclusive) have a very wrong theology of sports whereby they believe they must win all their matches before they could reflect God's glory. Even in the game of life, Christians do not win all the time; we win some and lose some. So is it with sporting activities also. Sports Ministry is not necessarily about winning the game but about participating in it for God's glory. In fact, Christians' definition of winning should be *"affecting lives positively for Christ"* or *"reforming the society for Christ through our participation in sport."* Therefore, Christians' attitudes in sports should not include 'it is either I win or you burst.' This is not godly. Stuart Weir, in one of his articles titled *God, Sport, Gold: A Christian view of Olympic*, put it correctly, "winning gold meant so much . . . yet for Christian, winning is not the sole point or aim of competing."[67] Christians athletes, coaches and/or spectators must do away with 'winning is everything' mentality. The fact is that, in the game of sports, somebody has to win and somebody has to lose; and there may be legitimate reasons for one's loss even as a Christian. Better still, the two teams (or sides) may even settle for a stalemate. In other words, the three possibilities in the outcome of sporting events are to win, to lose and to draw. Christians should be ready to accept any of the possible outcomes in good fate and with a large heart. Therefore, for the Christian athletes, if winning at all cost would bring shame and reproach to the name of Jehovah, one had better loose (or draw) than to win. After all, sport only has reward, per se, for the present life *"but godliness has value for all things, holding promise for both the present life and the life to come"* (1 Timothy 4:8).

CHAPTER NINE

STARTING SPORTS MINISTRY IN THE LOCAL CHURCH

The Sports Friends Nigeria, an arm of Sports Friends International with the International office in the USA, is a ministry of the multi-national interdenominational mission that is fully involved in Sports Ministry.[68] They have achieved the goals of evangelism, discipleship, and church planting (through sports), to some extent in South America, Asia and Africa.

In Africa, Sports Friends has ministry in the East, West and in the South. Nigeria is one of the nations that embraced the ministry of Sports Friends in West Africa.

In Nigeria also, they have achieved the goals of evangelism, discipleship and church planting (through sports) among some evangelical denominations like Evangelical Church Winning All (ECWA), Church of Christ in Nigeria (COCIN), and Ekkilisiyar Yan'uwa a Nigeria (meaning Church of the Brethren in Nigeria) among others[69] in the northern region of the nation.

Sports Friends has also extended its tentacles in collaboration with the Nigerian Baptist Convention in this creative athletic gospel. Incidentally, the Nigerian Baptist Convention's current theme, *Moving Forward with the Great Commission: Breaking New Frontiers* is in agreement with the vision of Sports Friends. Therefore, as a way of moving forward with the Great Commission through Sports Ministry, the following are my recommendations (as a sports minister) to all churches that would be considering starting a sports ministry:

Figure 6: How to Start Sports Ministry in the Local Church

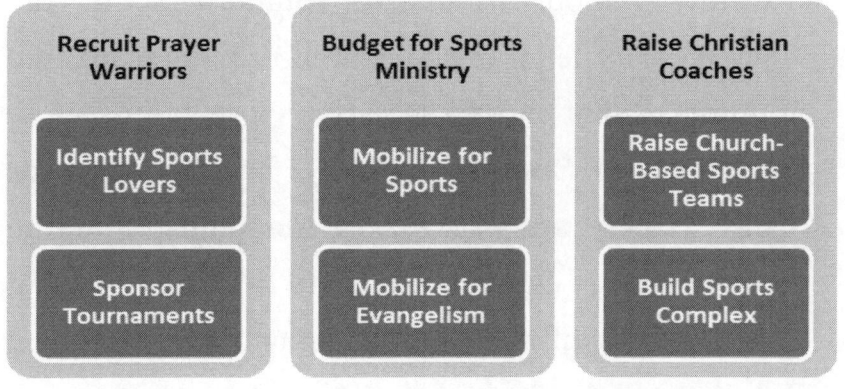

1. **Recruit Prayer Warriors:** In *Winning the World through Sports: The Role of the church*, this was my second recommendation, **but I was wrong**. Prayer is a very crucial point for every church that wants to embrace Sports Ministry and the church must consider it first. It is bedrock. Immediately the church catches the vision (Ezra 3:1), it is of necessity for church leaders to recruit prayer warriors before any other thing because sports can be risky for the growth and spiritual well-being of the church if there is no serious intercession. The outcome of the ministry may be devastating for the church in the end. In other words, without a sincere commitment of the intercessory team of the church in this regard, the church cannot have a successful Sports Ministry.
2. **Budget for Sports Ministry:** having prayed for the stability and success of the ministry in the church, the church needs to earmark certain percentages of the church annual budgets to be designated to Sports Ministry (Ezra 3:7). Sports

Friends International believes that it does not take much to start a Church-Centered Sports Ministry, yet the church must resolve to include the ministry in her annual finance. Unless the church is ready to support the ministry financially, she may not have a successful Sports Ministry.

3. **Raise Christian Coaches:** As I explained earlier, sports can be very dicey. Therefore, the church, through the pastor, would need to identify a sport-minded member who has a heart for ministry and delegate him/her to be in-charge of the ministry. Such an individual must be an adult and a maturing Christian, preferably not less than twenty years of age (Ezra 3:8). He or she should regularly report to the church pastor. However, there is need for the church to sponsor such a person for a series of training on how to use sports to do ministry inside and outside the church. Rodger Oswald referred to these Christian coaches as "shepherd-coaches"[70]. These people have both spiritual and athletic responsibilities. They carefully avoid over-

emphasizing athletic talents at the expense of Christ-likeness on the field of play.

4. **Identify Sports Lovers:** For the church to make impact in the world of sports, there are some people in the church who are really into sports; they just love it. The church, through the pastor and the shepherd-coach, should identify these people and designate them into the Sports Ministry team of the church.

5. **Mobilize for Sports:** Ordinarily, an average church member would think sport is only relevant for youths and students in the church. As much as this may be true, it is necessary for the church to also mobilize every church member (children, youths and adults) for sports. In other words, it is important for church members to exercise their bodies regularly for them to be sound and fit physically, psychologically, and with respect to health. Sport would also help to build good relationship among members of the same church.

6. Raise a Church-Based Sports Team: On this point, I acknowledge and appreciate the efforts of some churches that already have Church-Based football teams. However, these churches need to realize that football is not the only sport that the church can play. The church should identify the kind of sport that is predominant in her community and raise a Church-Based team for that sport. Rodger Oswald referred to this as resources survey.[71] This is the art of determining the sports interests of church members as well as members of the community.

In addition, this team must meet on weekly basis, for both training and interactions, which may not be more than 2 hours altogether.

A pastor approached me in one of the Sports Ministry vision castings that I went for sometimes ago. He said, he had noticed that the youths in the community of his church really love playing Table Tennis. Therefore, he intends to provide a Table

Tennis Board for them (in the church premises) that they may come around, play together and through that reach out to them with the Gospel of Jesus Christ.

7. **Sponsor Tournaments:** Occasionally, a group of churches in the same Association, Conference or even the Nigerian Baptist Convention (in our own case) may organize and sponsor tournaments in a particular community with the intention of winning souls for the Lord. On this point, I must clarify that the sole reason for Sports Ministry is not to organize tournaments and should not be mistaken for it. The sole reason is to raise God-fearing athletes from our churches to go into the outside world of sports and make a difference and a big impact to glorify God and win souls for the Lord.

8. **Mobilize for Evangelism:** This point and the previous one are inseparable. When these occasional tournaments are organized and sponsored, the evangelism team should be mobilized for witnessing and distribution of tracts

during sporting activities. In fact, it would be good if the Evangelism team and the Sports Ministry team of a local church could work in collaboration. Recently, I received invitation to watch a match between football teams of two Baptist churches in the city of Ibadan in Oyo State, Nigeria. While the match was going on, I overheard a discussion among some people who were also watching the match. I was very sad because one of them was counseling the others on how to visit whorehouses and Beer joints to *'enjoy'* themselves with their income in professional football. Immediately I heard this, I became uncomfortable and whispered to two of them to step out of the discussion. I spoke to them that what the other person was telling them was very wrong. I preached to and prayed with them while the match was still going on. I was glad because the Spirit of God convicted these young boys. This is exactly what churches should plan for whenever they are planning to stage a tournament. Mobilize for evangelism. I saw that opportunity as a teachable moment. Read more on teachable moment in the next chapter.

9. **Build Sports Complex:** This point should have come after the third point, Recruiting Christian Coaches; however, it is coming as the ninth point because of the financial implication attached to it. Not many local churches would be able to afford having a sport complex or a recreation center in the church premises. This point is actually for churches that are just starting on a new site; however, financially buoyant established churches can also consider it. The point here is that in this era of postmodernism, churches should plan for a sports complex on their sites. If the church plans her building structure with recreation ministry in mind, considering a sporting activity that were predominant in her community, non-Christians in that community would love to identify with the activities of the church. Note that if you won a soul for Christ through sport, you must be ready to keep the soul in the church through sport.

CHAPTER TEN

BASIC NEEDS FOR SPORTS MINISTRY

One of the reasons why some churches may not want to take the risk and responsibilities of Sports Ministry is the fear of the financial implications to sustain the ministry. It is important for the people running the affairs of the ministry in the church to understand the difference between **NEEDS** and **WANTS** of the ministry. I do not want to assume that every teaching and leadership in the ministry would be Bible-based. Hence, I have listed the Bible as a need for the ministry. Based on the submission of facilitators and delegates to the two Church-Centered Sports Ministry Basic Trainings held in the year 2013, for any local church to have a successful and sustainable sports ministry, the church should cater for the following:

Figure 7: Basic Needs for Sports Ministry

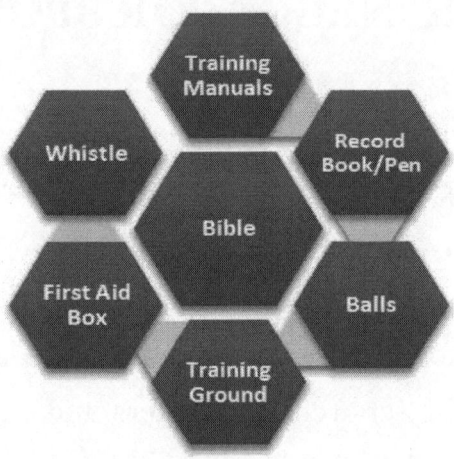

a. **Bible:** The word of God should be the Master manual and basis for any Sports Ministry of the local church. We cannot transform lives and reform the society except we keep the Word in our day-to-day involvements in the world.

b. **Training Manuals/Discipleship Books:** These are tools to help in mentoring and growing Christian athletes spiritually. The materials will also help them to understand how to go about managing the ministry.

c. **Note/Record book and Pen:** These would be used to record progress report of the team's activities. Rodger Oswald referred to these as forms and record keeping.[72]

d. **Balls:** For soccer, basketball, baseball, or handball depending on the kind of sport ministry the church intends to focus.

e. **Training Ground:** This is an alternative to building a Sports Complex. It could be in the church premises and/or in a near-by school playground. The church not having a training ground is not an acceptable excuse for not having a sports ministry in the local church. Church leaders could negotiate to use any playground around or in the neighborhood of the church.

f. **First Aid Box:** The life and well-being of the people in this ministry must be important to the church. Hence, the first aid box is a need.

g. **Whistle:** Helps in calling things to order in the team.

Leaders in the sports ministry unit of the local church should try to improvise for some other things the church may not be able to cater for at the start of the activities of the ministry in the church. This is a heart for ministry. Pastors and other leaders in the church should also try to encourage this ministry, as time goes on and as the church has the ability, by providing other needs of the team, not basic though. Some of this other needs include Training kits, cones, and incentives like energy drinks among others. This would also encourage sports ministry members to give their best.

Finally, as the church attempts to start a sports ministry, here are 'gentle warnings' or rules from Rodger Oswald to guide the church from committing error while starting the ministry

Figure 8: Guide to Error-Free Sports Ministry

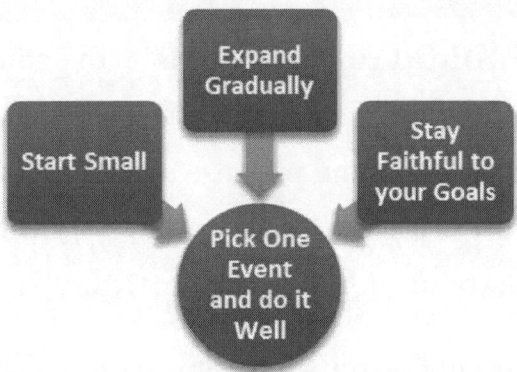

a. **Pick One Event/activity and do it well**: the local church Sports Ministry should start with just a single sporting activity. Too many sporting activities at a go may not be much effective and productive.

b. **Start Small**: the local church should not be afraid to start small. The church may not have all the resources for Sports Ministry at the out-set, but starting small is an asset for a successful ministry.

c. **Expand Gradually**: once the ministry is gaining acceptance in the church, then the church could consider combining more than one sporting activity on purpose.

d. **Stay Faithful to your Goals**[73]: the church pastor and shepherd-coach should be sensitive to run with the goals, vision and purpose of the ministry. This is because the Enemy would attack the ministry and attempt to turn it upside down.

Friend, I admonish you to accept and consider these recommendations as you intend to go beyond the four walls of your church in search for wandering souls in the world of sports for the Lord Jesus Christ.

CHAPTER ELEVEN

A CODED GOSPEL

Recently, I was on official assignment to my Alma Mata, the Nigerian Baptist Theological Seminary, Ogbomoso, and one of my lecturers (when I was a student there) raised an issue with me. He said, "Pastor Alabi, don't you think you should ask for a slot on the New Frontiers Television (the Television station of the Nigerian Baptist Convention) **to enlighten** the Baptist family on the subject of Sports Ministry?" I appreciated his concern because it would make the Sports Ministry to receive a wider coverage and acceptance, especially among the Nigerian Baptist Family. However, I told him that enlightening Christians on the subject of Sports Ministry through the Television station would defeat the purpose for starting the ministry. Of course, one could witness Christ **through** sports on air but it is not advisable in the contemporary Nigeria to enlighten Christians on air on **how to** use sports to witness to unbelievers.

Not quite long before the interaction with my lecturer, I was passing through a 'town' in Osun State and I noticed there was a traditional festival going on in the 'town'. What actually caught my attention was that among many activities outlined for the festival was a football competition tagged **"'Orisa Oloko' football competition"**. Immediately I saw this on the billboard, many thought ran through my mind at the same time. When the right set of people does not accept a vision, the wrong set of people is strategically positioned somewhere to destroy the vision. Imagine, when Christians are skeptical about penetrating the world through sports, idol worshippers are now organizing football competitions to celebrate their festivals! What an irony! Do we not think there is every possibility that teenagers who are supposed to be Christians would participate in such a competition? Would they not feel at home among these idol worshippers because of football more than they would do in the church?

SPORTS MINISTRY THROUGH MULTIMEDIA

There are different ways to preach the gospel; one of which is through sports on a multimedia. What actually matters while preaching the gospel through sports is for Christ-likeness to be demonstrated in our participation in sports, and this should be the emphasis of preachers on air. One could encourage Christian athletes to demonstrate the life and teachings of Christ on the field of play and encourage them to shine the light of Christ in the darkened world of sports. Jesus says,

> *"You are the light of the world. A town built on a hill cannot be hidden. Neither do people light a lamp and put it under a bowl. Instead, they put it on its stand, and it gives light to everyone in the house.* **In the same way, let your light shine before others, that they may see your good deeds and glorify your Father in heaven"** (Matthew 5:14-16; Emphasis mine).

The teaching in this passage should be the emphasis of the church as we intend to share the gospel through sports on the television. In the same way, churches may sponsor relaying of friendly matches among themselves on the television stations, however before this done, we must be sure the attitudes of these Christian footballers are not dishonorable to God.

CODING THE GOSPEL

Evangelism is becoming very difficult in Nigeria in this generation, particularly in the North. Christians are becoming more careful to share their faith because the world is now tending towards postmodernism and our national leaders are trying to promote all the religious sects in the nation, with a level of favoritism for Islam. Sports Ministry evolved essentially to make the gospel penetrate into the pluralistic religious community like ours via sporting activities, such that non-Christians or those who are hostile to the gospel would not be suspicious of our intention and enterprise. Apostle Paul says,

> *"Be wise in the way you act toward outsiders; make the most of every opportunity. Let your conversation be full of grace, seasoned with salt, so that you may know how to answer everyone"* (Colossians 4:4-6).

Sports Ministry is actually sports on the outside and ministry on the inside. It is to demonstrate the life and teachings of Jesus Christ –known as life-style evangelism- in whatever we do, especially on the field of play (Colossians 3:17).

Do we (as a church) think unbelievers would not someday rise to subvert our moves and intention if they eventually understand the motive behind our enterprise? Do we not think that **enlightening** Christians about Sports Ministry through television ministry (Multimedia) would rather be counter-productive? Counter-productive in the sense that both Christians and non-Christians have access to and could watch any Television program at any time. If the subject of a television program is about **how to** use sports to win souls for Christ and/or **how to** reach the unreached for the Lord through sports, non-Christians could also devise means to recruit rebels against the gospel through sports. We are all aware that some of these people derive pleasure in copying Christians.

TEACHABLE MOMENT

The challenge of relational evangelism and discipleship is actually on the shepherd-coach of the team who is expected to lead exemplary life. He/she is expected to demonstrate the gospel through his/her life-style to the children/teenagers in his/her team so that their lives too may be transformed for God's glory (1 Timothy 4:16). This implies that the coach would consciously live a Christian life until he/she gets a teachable moment to share the gospel. In the previous chapter, I spoke of the experience I had when I was invited to watch a football match between two Baptist Churches in Ibadan. That opportunity was a teachable moment personified.

Beth Lewis defined a teachable moment as "an unplanned opportunity that arises in the classroom where a teacher has an ideal chance to offer insight to his or her students." In this case, it is most likely to be on the playground between a Christian coach and the players in his team, especially after a training session. Lewis says, "Often it will require a brief digression that temporarily sidetracks the original lesson plan so that the teacher can explain a concept that has inadvertently captured the students' collective interest." What this implies is that if there was a conspicuous virtue (or vices) demonstrated by a player in the course of play, which raised an issue after the game, especially when the coach is addressing his/her players, the coach should use the opportunity as a teachable moment to share the gospel and emphasize the need to be born again. If there is no such opportunity, he/she should keep praying that such an opportunity might come, which would surely come on more than one occasion (Colossians 4:4-6).

Therefore, Sports Ministry in various local churches should be sensitive to the religious situation in Nigeria and devise means to share the gospel in a religiously porous society like ours. It is dangerous to enlighten Christians about how to go about operating Sports Ministry through Television programs or any form of multimedia because non-Christians could also watch the program and decode our coded gospel. However, it is not a bad idea to encourage Christian coaches, athletes, and spectators to distinguish themselves for the Lord in the world of sports through multimedia. Wherever it is an abomination to preach the gospel openly, Sports Ministry or the shepherd-coach should focus on prayer and building relationship with non-Christians in such community by having a sports team and/or a recreation center where people can come to interact and have 'fun' until there is a teachable moment when he could share the gospel without coercion. Ultimately, our life-styles as Christians in sports (as coaches, athletes and/or spectators) should demonstrate the gospel at all time.

CHAPTER TWELVE

UPHOLDING CHRISTIAN VIRTUES AS AN ATHLETE

Ricardo Izecson dos Santos Leite! Does that name sound familiar to you? Perhaps not!

What about the name '**Kaka**'? I guess everyone who loves soccer (football) is very familiar with that name.

Interestingly, the same person bears those names. The former is his real name while the latter is the name he chose to bear as a footballer.

Kaka is a relatively popular contemporary Brazilian footballer who presently plays for AC Milan Football Club in Italy after spending a few years with Real Madrid Football Club in Spain. He won the FIFA footballer of the year award in 2008.

Kaka became born again at the age of 12 and he is an evangelist on and off the football pitch. He is deeply involved with Evangelist Billy Graham Organization in a television campaign, which had an astonishing effect on Brazil. Kaka is used to having a white T-shirt under his jersey, especially during football match finals, with the inscription '*I belong to Jesus.*' He refused to have sex before his marriage to his wife, **Caroline**, which implies that he chose holiness unto God in the perverse world of sports. Kaka once said, *"I truly cannot imagine my life without Christ. Everything I have accomplished, everything I have done in my life was because God has a plan and a purpose for my life."*[74]

CHRISTIAN VIRTUES

Virtues are behavior or attitudes that show high moral standards as one relate to another. In other words, virtues focus on doing good and living quality life in the society. Unfortunately, they are becoming almost impossible in the world today, especially among athletes and/or sports lovers. They are being replaced with vices. If Christian virtues would be inscribed on the heart of athletes, it has to be from their childhood. In other words, churches should invest in Sports Ministry, and be concerned, especially with the children and teenagers in the church. This is the best period of human's life to bring him/her closer to God.

During the World War II, C. S. Lewis delivered a series of messages on virtues of life, and he gave the following, as reported by Steve Connor, as the seven virtues every Christian should possess to live a victorious Christian life: Prudence, Temperance, Justice, Fortitude, Faith, Hope and Love.[75]

- **Prudence**: this is being careful and sensible when one makes a decision.
- **Temperance**: this is ability to control one's behavior or attitude in a reasonable way.
- **Justice**: this is being fair in the way one treats others.
- **Fortitude**: this is when one is courageous in the face of great pain and great difficulties.
- **Faith**: it is to trust in somebody's ability or knowledge.

- **Hope**: it is to want something to happen and think that it is possible.
- **Love**: it is a strong feeling of deep affection for somebody or something, especially a member of one's family or a friend.

YOU ARE THE LIGHT OF THE WORLD

Christian athletes must always live and participate in sports with the consciousness of intentionally shinning the light of God. Jesus was not speaking to the Pharisees or those who did not believe in Him and His ministry; He was speaking to His disciples, referring to them as *"the light of the world."* In other words, Jesus Christ could not have been speaking to someone who has not confessed Him as Savior and Lord. Therefore, for athletes to be light of the world, he/she must be *born again.* Are you born again as an athlete? Could you vouch for the salvation of all athletes in your church's sports teams? Are you making efforts to lead children and teenagers in your church to Christ for greater exploit in the world?

Having accepted Jesus Christ as one's Savior and Lord, one needs to determine to be different for one's Savior and Lord in the midst of challenges and difficulties of the world. In other words, one must aspire to grow in the grace of God. Salvation experience is like a seed planted on a soil, and if not well nurtured, the seed would not grow to become a fruits-bearing tree. The fruit here is both internal and external fruits.

The internal fruit is the fruit of the Spirit as listed in Galatians 5:22-23: *"But the fruit of the Spirit is love, joy, peace, patience, kindness, goodness, faithfulness, gentleness, and self-control. Against such things there is no law."* As we bear the internal fruit in increasing measure, we bear the external fruits in return. In other words, the internal fruit begets the external fruits. The fruit of the Spirit is a pre-requisite for a fruitful Christian service. Apostle Peter says, *"For if you possess* **these qualities in increasing measure**, *they will keep you from being ineffective and unproductive in your* *knowledge of our Lord Jesus Christ"* (2 Peter 1:8; Emphasis mine).

External fruits are the souls we won for the Lord in the service we render to Him. Christian athletes are expected to influence the sporting world for the Lord so that through them, lives of unbelieving friends could be transformed for the glory of God. In other words, we become fruits-bearing trees for the Lord when we possess the qualities of the fruit of the Spirit in increasing measure.

UPHOLDING CHRISTIAN VIRTUES IN SPORTS

In the light of the foregoing, Christian athletes ought to uphold Christian virtues in sports. For instance

- **Prudence**: a maturing Christian athlete would be careful and sensible in his/her decision-making as regard issues in his/her participation in sports. What kind of decision do you take? A consciously growing Christian athlete would not allow the flesh and the world to be in charge in his/her life. Such will not allow sexual immorality and/or any form of impurity to defile and/or deface his/her body which is the temple of the Holy Spirit (1 Corinthians 3: 16).

- **Temperance**: Christian athletes must always be self-controlled. There are times when referees calls would warrant anger; the fact that one is a Christian should calm one down. This is not easy, but it is possible by the help of the Holy Spirit.
- **Justice**: Christian athletes must be fair in the way he/she treats fellow athletes and spectators. Such must treat every member in the team equally without being accused of favoritism.
- **Fortitude**: in the battle of life, it is normal to win some and lose some. So is it on the field of play. However, a Christian athlete should be courageous enough to accept (occasional) defeat and translate that spirit into the team.
- **Faith**: Christian athletes should be proud of their faith in God and be bold to tell their colleagues about the Lord Jesus Christ, in speech and indeed.

- **Hope**: Jesus Christ is coming again! Christian athletes should be hopeful for the Second coming of the Lord Jesus such that their participation in sports would not be a hindrance to their reign with God in His Kingdom.
- **Love**: a Christian athlete must love the Lord his God with all the heart, soul, mind, and strength (Mark 12:30) and endeavor to put God first in their participation in sport. That is when the entire world would *"see your good deeds and glorify your Father in heaven"*.

In other words, to uphold Christian virtues like Prudence, Temperance, Justice, Fortitude, Faith, Hope and Love in the world of sports, the church must

Figure 9: Upholding Christian Virtues in Athletes

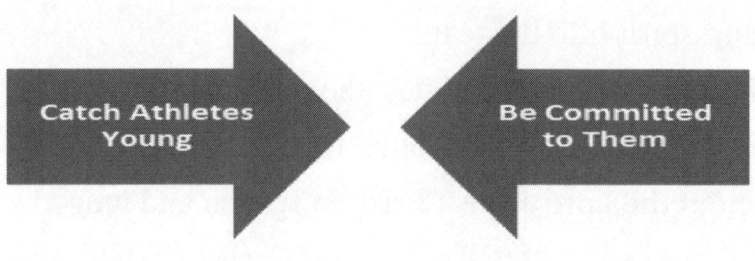

- ❖ **Catch these Athletes Young**: the church must ensure that athletes carrying her image and the image of Christ are born again from their childhood and/or teenage days. In addition, young non-Christian athletes in the church community must not be ignored or overlooked. This is very important for the church to help these athletes possess and uphold Christian virtues in sports.

- ❖ **Be committed to them**: the church must ensure that these athletes are nurtured to Christian maturity; they must be maturing Christians. There should be an intentional local church-based discipleship plan to encourage them to

    i. Pray without ceasing (1 Thess. 5:17),

    ii. Study the Bible diligently and regularly (Psalm 1:1-3),

    iii. Reject the influence of bad friends (2 Samuel 13; 2 Cor. 6: 14-18), and

iv. Live for God with perseverance in the midst of challenges and difficulties on daily basis (John 16:33).

Ricardo Izecson dos Santos Leite is a model for Christianity in the postmodern world of soccer (football) because he decided for the Lord Jesus at the tender age of twelve (12) and since then, he never looks back. He has been waxing stronger for the Lord on daily basis. He never jokes with his prayer life. **Kaka** never jokes with regular studying of the Bible. He never allows bad footballers to influence him, and he has been standing tall for the Lord in the corrupt world of footballers. Hence, God prospered his participation in football such that he was even adjudged the best footballer on the planet in the year 2008. What a shining light in the world of sports he is!

Catch athletes young and be committed to them as a Church.

CHAPTER THIRTEEN

REACTION TO SPORTING ACTIVITIES ON SUNDAYS

Walk down the street of any community in the Southwestern region of Nigeria on a Sunday morning, when adults (parents in most cases) are preparing to go or have gone to church for worship, and observe how many playgrounds you would see where young boys in their late teens and twenties gather to play certain number aside soccer. I know this is the case with almost all, if not all, regions in Nigeria, from the North to the South, to the East and to the West, though I would not like to be assertive.

During the week of the Centenary celebration of the Nigerian Baptist Convention in session in Ibadan, I met an elderly Seminary classmate at the venue who narrated his personal pastoral challenge to me with respect to young people playing sporting activities on Sunday mornings, especially when he learnt that I am presently into Sports Ministry. His church is sited in an area in Lagos State where majority living there are Muslims, hooked to playing football, even on Sunday mornings and would not want to have anything to do with the church. In the street of his church alone, there are about four different locations where these young boys would assemble concurrently on Sunday morning catching fun and enjoying themselves on the field of play. What a serious burden he has for these young ones.

I live close to a Deeper Life Bible Church and right beside the church when worship is ongoing on Sunday mornings, you would see these young boys playing a 5-aside football match. One would ask; how would church worship and football match be going on simultaneously in the same 'premises'? Do these youth have any form of reverence for God? How should the church react to this action of the youth?

I used to be in the category of these youth playing soccer on Sunday morning. Although, there was never a time (at least after my salvation experience) I went to do such a thing, I remember I did something related during the

World Cup played in Korea/Japan in the year 2002. Mind you, I was born again before that time. Due to difference in timing, (Korea and Japan's timing being GMT +9 while Nigeria is GMT +1) 8 hours difference, majority of the matches that were played in the evening in those two nations were played in the morning in Nigeria. One of the sixty-four football matches played in the competition involved a match between the Super Eagles of Nigeria and their counterparts from Argentina, the La Albiceleste. Incidentally, the match was to be played around 7 O' clock (Nigerian time) on a Sunday morning and I went to watch the match. Normally as an undergraduate that time, I preferred the first worship to the second one on Sundays, but on that day, I did not go for the first worship because of the football match. I actually went to church after the match; only that I attended the second service that started at 10 O'clock. Nevertheless, **I was wrong.** I was wrong because I missed the Sunday school that normally starts from 9 O'clock to 10 O'clock every Sunday morning. I was wrong because I did not put God first.

Sporting activities are not limited to Sunday mornings. There are other sporting activities, especially soccer/football in my context, that take place every Sunday afternoon and evening, such as the European leagues matches, Nigerian leagues matches and other local amateur matches in various communities in Nigeria. What is actually wrong with participating in sporting activities on Sunday, whether in the morning, afternoon, or in the evening?

On Sunday November 10, 2013, the pastor of my church announced to the congregation that there would be evening worship in the Church that day, as I believe many other pastors would have done. Normally, Sunday evening worship begins at 5pm in the Baptist denomination, where I fellowship, with discipleship life-style programme coming first and the evening worship coming next. Incidentally, there was going to be an English Premier League match between two giant clubs that have massive supports from among Nigerians at 5:10pm (kick off time); The Red Devils versus The Gunners at the Old Trafford stadium in the city of Manchester, United Kingdom. What a classic! I visited one of the football viewing centers around my house around that time and the crowd I saw there was much more than the number that normally attend the evening worship in my church. What a disaster that is for the church! What a challenge it is for Pastoral Ministry in Nigeria! How deserted lays the church in Nigeria and perhaps the church in the entire world!

> *"HOW DESERTED LIES THE CITY, ONCE SO FULL OF PEOPLE! HOW LIKE A WIDOW IS SHE, WHO ONCE WAS GREAT AMONG THE NATIONS! She who was queen among the provinces has now become a slave. Bitterly she weeps at night, tears are upon her cheeks. Among all her lovers there is none to comfort her; they have become her enemies. After affliction and harsh labour, Judah has gone into exile. She dwells among the nations; she finds no resting place. All who pursue her have overtaken her in the midst of her distress"* (Lamentations 1:1-3, Emphases mine).

I know the experience of your church is not likely to be different from the experience of my church every Sunday evening such that when there is even cell fellowship instead of the normal evening worship, the turnout of youth (especially boys and men) at this fellowship is not always encouraging. According to my submission in *Battle for the Nigerian Church,* the following are some of the effects of doing sporting activities on Sundays:

- ✓ Adverse Reduction in Church Attendance
- ✓ Withdrawal of Commitment to God through Church Activities
- ✓ Withdrawal of Financial Commitment to the Church
- ✓ Increase in Moral Decadence in the Society
- ✓ Evil means of Making Money
- ✓ Absent Mindedness in the Church

What then should the church do to reduce this havoc done on the church? There are three major and complimentary things the church needs to do to come out of this predicament and according to Rodger Oswald[76], they are to:

1. Reach Up
2. Reach In
3. Reach Out

Figure 10: The Right Way to Participate in Sports

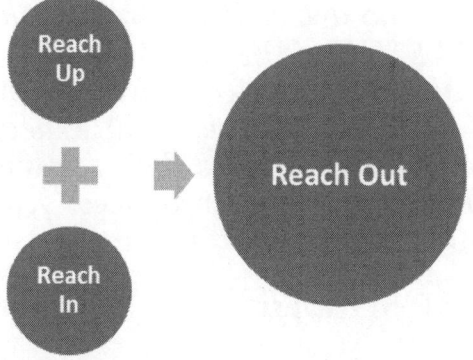

I.   REACH UP

The number one reaction of the church to playing sporting activities on Sundays is to return to God in prayer. The heart of the postmodern youth is far away from God, and the prayer life of the contemporary church is less effective. Perhaps we make so much noise as a body of believers without really praying the

Bible way. We need to return to God and commit the hearts of our youth to the hand of God. Every church should be committed to prayer focusing on minimizing and removing of the negative effects of sporting activities on the church, and participate in sport in a responsible and God-glorifying way. The Bible says,

> *"If my people, who are called by my name, WILL HUMBLE THEMSELVES AND PRAY AND SEEK MY FACE AND TURN FROM THEIR WICKED WAYS, then will I hear from heaven and will forgive their sin and will heal their land"* (2 Chronicles 7:14, Emphasis mine).

Perhaps we need to realize that prayerlessness is wickedness in the sight of God. The church's prayerlessness is wickedness before God, and the Christians' over-indulgence to sporting activities is wickedness in the sight of God. Hence, the Lord admonished the church as He admonished the Israel of old to seek Him in humility of heart and turn from her wicked ways —both the leaders and members of the church. Ask the Lord to turn the hearts of the youth to Him. We need to Reach Up!

II. REACH IN

It is rather unfortunate that the contemporary church has so many undiscipled members fellowshipping together in the same Body, yet we claim to have discipleship program in our churches. Our discipleship network program seems to be less effective on the lives of church members. Perhaps our discipleship program is more of academic than relationship such that the lives of the so-called disciple makers (or disciplers) are not worthy of emulation. Therefore, the contemporary church needs to re-strategize and nurture the seed of Christianity planted in the hearts of men (generic) at salvation. While discussing this point in *Battle for the Nigerian Church,* I noted that this 'reaching in' must result in the following in the lives of individual believer in Christ, irrespective of age or number of years that one had been saved:

Figure 11: Result of Discipleship

- ➢ **Love for God**: correct and proper discipleship would help a Christian to have the right perspective of loving the Lord (Deuteronomy 6: 4-9).

- ➢ **Gratitude Attitude**: an attitude of gratitude would help the Christian prioritize his/her participation in sporting activities or any secular activity whatsoever because we are saved to serve and worship the Lord. All other things are secondary (Exodus: 3:12).

> **Holiness unto the Lord**: holiness in this context implies outgrowing the stage of ignorance (1 Peter 1: 14-16). We outgrow our spiritual ignorance through consistent transformation and we become more like Jesus Christ through relational discipleship.

> **Commitment to God**: this was not included in my points in *Battle for the Nigerian Church*, but of a truth, when one is properly discipled, one would be properly committed to God, to His children, and to His work. This work of God includes ministering to non-Christians.

III. REACH OUT

This is the last reaction the Lord is expecting from the church with respect to sporting activities on Sundays, and we should not be afraid to embark on it, especially through the efforts of well discipled Christian athletes in various churches. It is the follow-on of our reaching up and reaching in. Permit me to lift this section almost verbatim from the booklet *Battle for the Nigerian Church*.

Sunday, which is the Lord's Day, has replaced the Sabbath in our contemporary time to honour the resurrection of Jesus Christ, and I have rightly explained that it is wrong to participate in Sports at the expense of our worship to God. However, there is another dimension to participation in sports on the Lord's Day. The Bible says,

> *"Going on from that place, (Jesus) went into their synagogue, and a man with a shriveled hand was there. Looking for a reason to accuse Jesus, they asked Him, 'Is it lawful to heal on the Sabbath?' He said to them, 'if any of you has a sheep and falls into a pit on the sabbath, will you not take hold of it and lift it out? How much valuable is a man than a sheep! Therefore, it is lawful to do good on the sabbath'"* (Matthew 12: 9-12).

According to the passage, Jesus says, it is *lawful* to take hold of anybody that falls into a pit and lift him/her out, even on Sundays. That is my interpretation of Matthew 12: 9-12.

On Sunday morning when youth pay allegiance to sports and fun, while Christian faithful choose service and worship to God, to Jesus, they are sheep who have fallen into the pit, and the Lord says, it is lawful for the church, His contemporary disciples, to look out for them and lift them out of the pit. On Sunday evening when millions of youth decide to watch or play sport at the expense of worship, to Jesus, they are sheep who have fallen into the pit, and the Lord says,

> *"I have OTHER SHEEP that are not of this sheep pen. I must bring them also. They too will listen to my voice, and there shall be one flock and one shepherd"* (John 10:16, Emphasis mine).

I need to confess now that this is a very delicate assignment; however, if it were not possible, Jesus would not ask the church to do it. Nevertheless, the task is not necessarily meant for every member of the church, but for the Sports Ministry team or Sports Evangelists of the church.

The team should build intentional relationship with the lost, which focuses on doing good and living good, such that team members' lifestyles could attract spiritual curiosity which bring the unbelievers to the Lord Jesus (Matthew 5:16).[77] After all, Christianity is not a religion, but a three-dimensional relationship (a relationship to God, to fellow Christians and to non-Christians).

Figure 12: Christianity as a 3D-Relationship

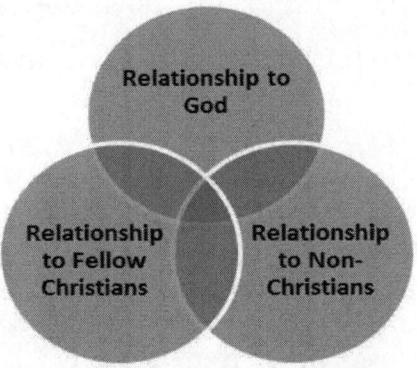

In other words,

    a. This form of evangelism is relational, friendship and/or lifestyle evangelism. The team would build intentional relationship with the lost.

b. The Sports Ministry must accept this privilege as a call to Christian service. Not every Christian can be a sports evangelist but every Christian should be a relational evangelist in one way or the other, not necessarily through sports evangelism. Some sports evangelists are regarded as coaches (sports coaches) in some places in the Northern Nigeria.[78]

c. These evangelists must watch their lives closely such that they do not become victims of the Devil instead of being victors. This implies that the spiritual lives of every member of the Sports Ministry must be burning for the Lord. If they would go 'afishing' on any particular Sunday, they must have first been with God (individually and corporately), receive instruction from Him before going out to rescue the lost.

d. This team must operate in agreement with the church's vision and purpose. In other words, the church must be aware of any and every of their activities by regularly reporting to the pastor of the local church for necessary assistance to come from the church.

e. The church, through the team leader (shepherd-coach), should have a target group and be creative in carrying out the assignment. This creativity could involve the church also having a soccer-viewing center or a recreation center, open to all people, but targeting the lost. At half time of every match, there could be a brief sermon for viewers or somebody delegated to distribute tracts to viewers. This viewing center or recreation center would invariably function, as a ministry arm of the church, especially to the lost, and it should be closed down or locked up at every hour of worship (mid-week programs inclusive) and encourage regular viewers or users (as the case may be) to join in worship. Another thing that could be peculiar with this viewing center is that the church should subsidize for the viewing price per match as a way to attract or invite sport lovers to the center.

Some churches are even capable of making it free of charge. This viewing center should also not tolerate gambling or any practice of social vices in order to encourage Christian morality and virtues among viewers.

Alternatively, the church could encourage her members running personal soccer-viewing centers to maintain their stand for Christ and use the opportunity for mission as much as for financial gain –witnessing to their customers in whichever way and discouraging every form of social vices in their viewing centers to encourage Christian virtues.

In all, the leadership of the church should allow the Holy Spirit to be in-charge of this commission that the church may regularly receive new insight from the Lord on how to run the affairs of the ministry creatively (1 John 2:27).

CONCLUSION

"I am not astonished that you are so quickly deserting Him who called you in the grace of Christ and are turning to a different gospel ... As we have said before, so now I say again: If anyone is preaching to you a gospel contrary to the one you received, let him be accursed " (Galatians 1:6-9).

So far so good, this book has examined three sections that considered the subjects of Sports, Sports Ministry and the Role of the church in Sports Ministry. It has examined definitions of Sports and Sports Ministry, the historical backgrounds of Sports and Sports Ministry, Theology of Sports, Philosophy, Vision, Mission, and Purpose of Sports Ministry among other ones. It also explicitly examined the Role of the Church in using sport as a tool for soul winning, with more emphasis on football (soccer). In all, this is not an attempt to teach a gospel contrary to the Gospel of the Lord Jesus, but to present it in a manner that would help the church to cater for the unchurched (non-Christians), particularly the un-churched athletes.

In the real sense of the word, sport is neutral; it is neither good nor bad and it is either good or bad. The person of the coach, athlete and/or spectator would determine how good or bad sports would be. Similarly, one could be either wrong or right to participate in sport, depending on the place of God in one's heart, and depending on the purpose for which one is involved in it.

I must confess also that sports could be very dicey if there is no conviction and proper plan before one venture into using it for ministry purpose. The pastor needs to get the vision for sports ministry right, set goals for the church and purposefully pursue the goal to the glory of God and the expansion of His Kingdom here on earth. In the case whereby the pastor does not have the vision for Sports Ministry, he/she should support the vision if there is any member of the church suggesting it as a ministry arm of the church. Remember, Christianity is a three-dimensional relationship —to God, to fellow Christians and to non-Christians. It involves your relationship to sports and sports addicts.

It is time for us to be contemporary as a church rather than being conservative. It is time for us to see ministry beyond the four walls of the local church and extend ministry into the midst of sports enthusiasts. It is time for us to see beyond the challenges sports may be posing for the church and intentionally re-strategize how we can turn this *'stumbling block'* called sports into *'a stepping stone'* for soul winning, discipleship, church growth and church planting. Jesus Christ is the Lord, even in the stadium!

APPENDIX

HOW TO START SPORTS MINISTRY IN SCHOOLS

I was required to write a proposal for a higher institution of learning on "How to Start a Sports Ministry in the School", and the following are my suggestions for consideration. Mind you, these suggestions are applicable to both Secondary Schools and Tertiary institutions. Private Elementary schools may also find it useful, especially now that sporting academy is becoming popular with Nigerians. Sports Ministry can only function and be productive in the school where the management and Chaplaincy understand the concept and work in collaboration with the ministry. The ministry could even be an arm of the Chaplaincy. We need to make efforts to make Jesus Christ known to this generation. The suggestions are:

- ✓ **Recruit Prayer Warriors**: this would be made easier in collaboration with the School Chaplaincy.

It is so important that without it, the ministry is not likely to be successful in the school.

✓ **Budget for Sports**: this school management should earmark a certain percentage annually in the School budget. This is important for the project/vision to be realistic.

✓ **Recruit Christian Coaches**: this could also be part of the budget or financial implications. The school management needs to employ professionally trained coaches who also have hearts for ministry. Unless the coaches are Shepherd-coaches, their employment is likely to defeat the purpose of the ministry.

✓ **Build Sports Complex**: this may not come up immediately after recruiting the Christian Coaches, however, because of its importance; the school management should survey a playground for a start, plan to build a Sports Complex and work towards it.

However, it is necessary to start with relevant sporting equipment.

- ✓ **Identify Athletes**: there are students who are naturally gifted athletes; it is one of the responsibilities of these coaches to discover their potentials and develop them.

- ✓ **Raise Sports Teams**: there are different kinds of sporting activities in the world, but only few are popular with Nigerians. Check them out in chapter three of this book. It is also one of the responsibilities of these coaches to raise teams for different sporting activities and meet regularly for training on the playground or in the Sports Complex, as the case may be.

- ✓ **Associate with Other Schools**: Christianity is not a religion, but a relationship. Therefore, the school management should identify with other schools by engaging them in friendly or competitive sporting activities. It is through this that Christian athletes could manifest the light of the world and the salt of the earth that Christ claims they are (Matthew 5:14-16).

- ✓ **Mobilize for Evangelism**: as it is normal for every sporting team to have a supporters' club, so is it necessary for the school to have one. However, this supporters' club is actually meant for mission and evangelism. As the school goes out for either competitive or friendly sporting events, this club/team would also go with them with tracts and necessarily carry 'the banner of Christ' in the stadium. The mindset of this club is not necessarily to win games at all cost but to win souls for the Lord. However, the athletes should be encouraged to excel in their participation in sports to the glory of God and the expansion of His Kingdom on earth.

Do you have any questions or you need any clarifications on this book?

Do you need a seminar or workshop on this book?

Write, Call or Contact the author

Pastor Samuel Ayantoye ALABI

Sports Ministry Unit, Youth & Students Ministries Department, Nigerian Baptist Convention, P. M. B. 5113, Baptist Building, Ibadan, Nigeria.

+2348030497794 and +2348159990308

E-mail: <u>samalbs0881@gmail.com</u>

Facebook: Samuel Ayantoye Alabi

Twitter: @SamuelAyantoyeA

"I am entrusted with the gospel to the uncircumcised" Galatians 2:7-8.

Other Books by the Author

1. Die to Sin and Save the Church (2008)

2. Living against Odds of Life (2010)

3. Winning the World through Sports (2013)

4. How to make Right Decisions (2013)

5. Battle for the Nigerian Church (2014)

INDEX

A

AC Milan Football Club	113
Alexander Cartwright	33
Ancient Greece	30
Ancient Olympic Games	30, 63
Athletes	86, 116
Athletics	44
Athletic Gospel	91, 108

B

Badminton	44
Baseball	33
Basic Needs for Sports Ministry	100
Basketball	44
Beth Lewis	110
Biblical Antecedents to Sport	61, 62
Born Again	116

C

C. S. Lewis	115
Changing Times Period	32
Charles Kingsley	64, 65
Chess	44
Christ Apostolic Church Grammar School	70
Christian Virtues in Sports	118, 119, 120

Christmanship	55
Church-Based Sports Team	95
Church-Centered Sports Ministry	93
Church Fathers	62
Church Growth	142
Church Planting	142
Church of Christ in Nigeria	90
Clifford Putney	65
Coach	93
Coding the Gospel	108
Cricket	45

D

David W. Cunningham	85
Deeper Life Bible Church	124
Definition of Sports	28
Definition of Sports Ministry	52, 53
Different Kinds of Sports	38
Discipleship	59, 87
Discipleship Life-Style Programme	22, 126
Doctrine of Dualism	24, 63

E

'Ekkilisiyar Yan'uwa a' Nigeria	90, 91
Emperor Theodosius	31, 63
English Football League	34
English Premier League	126
European Leagues Matches	126

Evangelical Church Winning All   90
Evangelist Billy Graham Organization   113
External Fruits   117

F

FIFA   35
FIFA Footballer of the Year Award 113
FIFA World Cup   35, 125
Football   45
Friendship Evangelism   136
Fulham Football Club   65

G

God's Kingdom   141
Gospel   67, 107
Greek Boxers   30

H

Handball   45
Hanoverian Period   32
History of FIFA   35
History of Sports   30
History of Sports Ministry   61
Hockey   45

I

Ibadan Baptist Conference   97
Incarnation Evangelism   136
Internal Fruit   117
Islam   108

J

James Naismith	34
Jerusalem Temple	49
John Garner	63
Judo	45

K

Kaka	113, 122

L

Leisure	27
Lifestyle Evangelism	136
Lists of Some Sports Ministries	68
Local Amateur Matches	126

M

Martin Luther	63, 64
Maturing Christian	117
Media	21
Medieval Period	31
Minimester Programme	23
Ministry of Reconciliation	51, 52
Missionary Agencies	69
Muscular Christianity	64, 65
Muscular Missionaries	65
Music	21
Muslims	71

N

National Sports Policy of Nigeria	28

New Frontiers Television 105
New York Knickerbockers 33
Nigerian Baptist Convention 90
Nigerian Baptist Pastors 23
Nigerian Baptist Theological Seminary, Ogbomoso 23, 105
Nigerian Leagues Matches 126
Nigerian Universities Games Association 44
Northern Nigeria 137

O

Old Trafford Stadium 126
Olympic Games 30
Orange African Cup of Nations 22
'Orisa Oloko' Football Competition 106

P

Pastoral Ministry in Nigeria 126
Practical Theology 23

Q

Queens Park Rangers Football Club 65

R

Real Madrid Football Club 113
Recreation Center 137
Recreation Ministry 51, 63
Reformation Period 63
Relational Discipleship 87, 131
Relational Evangelism 133
Ricardo Izecson dos Santos Leite 113, 122

Rodger Oswald	78, 129
Royal Ambassador of Nigeria	70

S

Sabbath	134
Second World War	67
Shah Mat	31
Shepherd-Coaches	93, 138
Soccer-Viewing Center	138
Soul Winning	87
South African Theological Seminary	23
Southampton Football Club	65
Southwestern Region of Nigeria	123
Spectator	88
Sports Evangelism	138
Sports Friends International	92, 93
Sports Friends Nigeria	90
Sports Ministry through Multimedia	107
Sportsology	85
Stepping Stone	142
Steve Connor	76
Stuart Weir	88
Stumbling Block	142
Sunday school	125
Super Eagles of Nigeria	22, 125
Swimming	46

T

Table Tennis	46
Taekwondo	46
Teachable Moment	110
Tennis	46
The Great Commission	91
The Gunners	126
The Holy Spirit	139
The Lord's Day	134
The Middle Ages	62
The Period of Tudor and Stuart	32
The Red Devils	126
Thomas Hughes	65
Timothy Tucker	23, 52
Traditional Activities	31

V

Volleyball	47

W

William McGregor	33, 34

Y

Youth	21

BIBLIOGRAPHY

Alabi, Samuel A. *Battle for the Nigerian Church*. Nigeria: Abbey Business Concept, Mokola, Ibadan, January 2014.

_____ *Muscular Christianity: Rebuilding the Broken Wall of Relational Evangelism in Nigeria*. An unpublished paper written for Sports Ministry Unit, Youth & Students Ministries Department of the Nigerian Baptist Convention, November 5, 2013.

_____ *Winning the World through Sports: The Role of the Church*. Nigeria: Abbey Business Concept, Mokola, Ibadan, April 2013.

Armstrong, G. and Giulianotti, R. (eds.) *Football in Africa*. New York: Palgrave Macmillan, 2004.

Audu, Musa D. U. *NUGA: The Road to Excellence* Nigeria: Ahmadu Bello University Press Limited, Zaria, Kaduna State, 2013.

Cochrane, Lyn *Building Bridges and Connecting People to the Local Church*, A handbook of The Salvation Army Australia Southern Territory Sports Ministry, n. d.

Connor, Steve *Sports Outreach: Principles and Practice for Successful Sports Ministry*. Ross-shire, Scotland: QUE, 2003

Garner, John (ed.) *Recreation and Sport Ministry: Impacting Postmodern Culture*. Nashville: Broadman & Holman, 2003.

Gin, Valerie J. and McCown, Laurie *Focus on Sport in Ministry*. Marietta, GA: QUE, 2003

http://en.wikipedia.org/wiki/History_of_sport

http://www.fifa.com/classicfootball/history/fifa/foundation.html retrieved on 07/24/2013

http://www.hhp.txstate.edu/hper/faculty/pankey/1310/ch17Bread.htm

http://www.historyworld.net/wrldhis/PlainTextHistories.asp?ParagraphID=bue

http://www.sportscommission.gov.ng/national_sports_policy.pdf

www.en.wikipedia.org/wiki/William_McGregor

www.topendsports.com/sport/sport-list.htm

Ladd, Tony and Mathisen, Jim A. *Muscular Christianity*. Grand Rapids, MU: Baker Books, 1999.

Mackenzie, B. *History of Sport and Games.* 2004 Available from: http://www.brianmac.co.uk/history.htm

Mary Bellis. http://inventors.about.com/od/sstartinventions/tp/History-Of-Sports.htm

MedicineNet.com, *Health Benefits of Physical Activity*, www.medicinenet.com/script/main/art.asp?articlekey=10074

Oakley, Dave *Why Sport?* Report compiled for Ambassadors in Sport: 2003.

Oswald, Rodger *Starting a Sports Ministry in the Local Church*, A Manual prepared by Church Sports International, 2001.

Parker, Andrew and Collins, Mike *Sport and Christianity in the 21st Century.* Encounter Mission Journal, University of Gloucestershire, Issue 41 July 2012.

Phillips, Patrick et al (ed.) *Oxford Advanced Learner's Dictionary of Current English* International Student's Edition. New York: Oxford University Press, 2010.

Putney, Clifford *Muscular Christianity: Manhood and Sports in Protestant America, 1880 – 1920.* Boston: Harvard University Press. 2001.

Sports Friends Training Manual, *Church-Centered Sports Ministry,* Participants' Manual for Basic Training, Revised in March 2010.

Tucker, Timothy *A Strategy for the Development of a Sustainable Sports Ministry Using Mission Outreach through Soccer in Selected Churches in Tshwane.* An Unpublished Master of Theology Thesis in Practical Theology, submitted to the South African Theological Seminary on June 2011.

_____ *Introduction to Sports Ministry.* A publication of the South African Theological Seminary. 2009.

Tucker, Tim and Woodbridge, Noel *A Strategy for Developing a Sustainable Sports Ministry through Soccer Evangelism in the Local Churches in Tshwane Using Browning's Multidisciplinary Model*, n. d.

Watson, Nick J. et al, *The Development of Muscular Christianity in Victorian Britain and Beyond.* Journal of Religion and Society, Volume 7, ISSN 1522-5658, 2005.

White, Matthew Brian. *Sports Ministry in America's One Hundred Largest Churches.* An Unpublished Dissertation Presented to the Faculty of Asbury Theological Seminary USA in Partial Fulfillment of the Requirement for the Degree of Doctor of Ministry, May 2006.

NOTES

[1] www.en.wikipedia.org/wiki/Sport retrieved on 09/12/2012 at 11:09pm

[2] Tony Ladd and Jim A. Mathisen. *Muscular Christianity*. Grand Rapids, MU: Baker Books, 1999.

[3] www.en.wikipedia.org/wiki/Sport retrieved on 09/12/2012 at 11:09pm

[4] Ibid

[5] http://www.sportscommission.gov.ng/national_sports_policy.pdf

[6] www.en.wikipedia.org/wiki/Sport retrieved on 09/12/2012 at 11:09pm

[7] Mary Bellis. http://inventors.about.com/od/sstartinventions/tp/History-Of-Sports.htm

[8] http://www.historyworld.net/wrldhis/PlainTextHistories.asp?ParagraphID=bue

[9] http://en.wikipedia.org/wiki/History_of_sport

[10] http://www.historyworld.net/wrldhis/PlainTextHistories.asp?groupid=2274&HistoryID=ac02&gtrack=pthc

[11] Ibid

[12] Ibid

[13] Ibid

[14] Ibid

[15] Ibid

[16] B. Mackenzie. *History of Sport and Games*. 2004 Available from: http://www.brianmac.co.uk/history.htm [Accessed 23/7/2013]

[17] Ibid

[18] Ibid

[19] Ibid

[20] http://www.hhp.txstate.edu/hper/faculty/pankey/1310/ch17Bread.htm

[21] Ibid

[22] Mary Bellis. http://inventors.about.com/od/sstartinventions/tp/History-Of-Sports.htm

[23] www.en.wikipedia.org/wiki/William_McGregor retrieved on 03/14/2013 at 8:44pm

[24] Ibid

[25] Steve Connor. *Sports Outreach: Principles and Practice for Successful Sports Ministry*. Ross-shire, Scotland: QUE, 2003

[26] Ibid

[27] Tim Tucker. *Introduction to Sports Ministry*. A publication of the South

Africa Theological Seminary. 2009.

[28] B. Mackenzie. *History of Sport and Games*. 2004 Available from: http://www.brianmac.co.uk/history.htm [Accessed 23/7/2013]

[29] http://www.fifa.com/classicfootball/history/fifa/foundation.html retrieved on 07/24/2013 at 12:03pm

[30] B. Mackenzie. *History of Sport and Games*. 2004 Available from: http://www.brianmac.co.uk/history.htm [Accessed 23/7/2013]

[31] http://www.fifa.com/classicfootball/history/fifa/foundation.html retrieved on 07/24/2013 at 1:03pm

[32] Ibid

[33] B. Mackenzie. *History of Sport and Games*. 2004 Available from: http://www.brianmac.co.uk/history.htm [Accessed 23/7/2013]

[34] Ibid

[35] Matthew Brian White *Sports Ministry in America's One Hundred Largest Churches* A Dissertation Presented to the Faculty of Asbury Theological Seminary in Partial Fulfillment of the Requirement for the Degree of Doctor of Ministry, May 2006.

[36] Musa D. U. Audu *NUGA: The Road to Excellence* Nigeria: Ahmadu Bello University Press Limited, Zaria, Kaduna State, 2013, pp. 35-36

[37] Tim Tucker. *Introduction to Sports Ministry.* A publication of the South African Theological Seminary. 2009, pp. 147 – 153.

[38] Ibid, p. 25

[39] Timothy Tucker. *A Strategy for the Development of a Sustainable Sports Ministry Using Mission Outreach through Soccer in Selected Churches in Tshwane.* An Unpublished Master of Theology Thesis submitted to the South African Theological Seminary on June 2011.

[40] MedicineNet.com, *Health Benefits of Physical Activity.* www.medicinenet.com/script/main/art.asp?articlekey=10074, retrieved on 10/03/2013 at 11:04am.

[41] Steve Connor. *Sports Outreach: Principles and Practice for Successful Sports Ministry.* Ross-shire, Scotland: QUE, 2003

[42] Timothy Tucker. *A Strategy for the Development of a Sustainable Sports Ministry Using Mission Outreach through Soccer in Selected Churches in Tshwane.* An Unpublished Master of Theology Thesis submitted to the South African Theological Seminary on June 2011.

[43] Rodger Oswald, *Starting a Sports Ministry in the Local Church,* A Manual prepared by Church Sports International, 2001.

[44] This was not originally in the four given by Major Lyn Cochrane of the Salvation Army, Australia; it was included during my interaction with Rev Mrs. Foluke Ola in my office.

[45] Lyn Cochrane, *Building Bridges and Connecting People to the Local Church,* A handbook of The Salvation Army Australia Southern Territory Sports Ministry, n. d.

[46] Tim Tucker and Noel Woodbridge in *A Strategy for Developing a*

[47] Ibid

[48] John Garner (ed.) *Recreation and Sport Ministry: Impacting Postmodern Culture.* Nashville: Broadman & Holman, 2003.

[49] http://www.historyworld.net/wrldhis/PlainTextHistories.asp?groupid=2274&HistoryID=ac02&gtrack=pthc

[50] John Garner (ed.) *Recreation and Sport Ministry: Impacting Postmodern Culture.* Nashville: Broadman & Holman, 2003., pg 40.

[51] Andrew Parker and Mike Collins. *Sport and Christianity in the 21st Century.* Encounter Mission Journal, University of Gloucestershire, Issue 41 July 2012.

[52] Clifford Putney. *Muscular Christianity: Manhood and Sports in Protestant America, 1880 – 1920.* Boston: Harvard University Press. 2001, p 11.

[53] Nick J. Watson et al, *The Development of Muscular Christianity in Victorian Britain and Beyond.* Journal of Religion and Society, Volume 7 (2005), ISSN 1522-5658.

[54] Andrew Parker and Mike Collins. *Sport and Christianity in the 21st Century.* Encounter Mission Journal, University of Gloucestershire, Issue 41 July 2012.

[55] Dave Oakley. *Why Sport?* Report compiled for Ambassadors in Sport: 2003.

[56] Tim Tucker and Noel Woodbridge. *A Strategy for Developing a Sustainable Sports Ministry through Soccer Evangelism in the Local Churches in Tshwane Using Browning's Multidisciplinary Model.*

[57] G. Armstrong and R. Giulianotti (eds.) *Football in Africa.* New York: Palgrave Macmillan. 2004, p 8.

[58] Tim Tucker. *Introduction to Sports Ministry.* A publication of the South African Theological Seminary. 2009, p 48.

[59] Tim Tucker and Noel Woodbridge. *A Strategy for Developing a Sustainable Sports Ministry through Soccer Evangelism in the Local Churches in Tshwane Using Browning's Multidisciplinary Model.*

[60] Gin, Valerie J. and Laurie McCown. *Focus on Sport in Ministry.* Marietta, GA: QUE, 2003

[61] Tim Tucker. *Introduction to Sports Ministry.* A publication of the South Africa Theological Seminary. 2009, pp. 147 – 153.

[62] Steve Connor. *Sports Outreach: Principles and Practice for Successful Sports Ministry.* Ross-shire, Scotland: QUE, 2003

[63] Ibid

[64] Rodger Oswald, *Starting a Sports Ministry in the Local Church*, A Manual prepared by Church Sports International, 2001.

[65] www.sports4him.org/home retrieved on 09/12/2012 at 10:31pm

[66] Ibid

[67] www.veritesport.co.uk retrieved on 09/12/2012 at 10:24pm

[68] Sports Friends Training Manual, *Church-Centered Sports Ministry,* Basic Training Participants' Manual, revised in March 2010.

[69] I knew this through my interaction and collaborative work with the Sports Friends, Nigeria Team.

[70] Rodger Oswald, *Starting a Sports Ministry in the Local Church*, A Manual prepared by Church Sports International, 2001.

[71] Ibid

[72] Ibid

[73] Ibid

[74] www.blog.hardkop.com/index.php/posts retrieved on 03/18/2013 at 9:46pm

[75] Steve Connor. *Sports Outreach: Principles and Practice for Successful Sports Ministry.* Ross-shire, Scotland: QUE, 2003

[76] Rodger Oswald, *Starting a Sports Ministry in the Local Church*, A Manual prepared by Church Sports International, 2001.

[77] Samuel A. Alabi. *Muscular Christianity: Rebuilding the Broken Wall of Relational Evangelism in Nigeria.* A paper written for the Sports Ministry Unit, Youth & Students Ministries Department of the Nigerian Baptist Convention, November 5, 2013.

[78] I knew this through my interaction with Pastor Jonah H. Yila, a colleague in the ministry from Gombe State, Nigeria.

Printed in Great Britain
by Amazon.co.uk, Ltd.,
Marston Gate.